The Cubic Curriculum

The Cubic Curriculum

E.C. WRAGG

London and New York

First published 1997
by Routledge
11 New Fetter Lane, London EC4P 4EE

Simultaneously published in the USA and Canada
by Routledge
29 West 35th Street, New York, NY 10001

Typeset in Sabon by Solidus (Bristol) Limited

Printed and bound by Bath Press

British Library Cataloguing in Publication Data

A catalogue record for this book is available from the British Library

Library of Congress Cataloging in Publication Data

Wragg, E.C. (Edward Conrad)
    The cubic curriculum/E.C. Wragg.
        p.   cm.
    Includes bibliographical references and index.
    ISBN (invalid) 0–415–14311–1 (pbk. : alk. paper)
    1. Education—Great Britain—Curricula.   2. Curriculum
development—Great Britain.   3. Curriculum change—Great Britain.
I. Title.
LB1564.G7W73   1996   96–33060
375 '.00941–dc20   CIP

ISBN 0–415–14341–1

Contents

Illustrations

THINK BOXES

Preface

This book is based on a series of lectures I have given on education for the future. As the twenty-first century approached there were many speculations about what life might hold for young people now in school. I found myself wondering whether a curriculum that was seen mainly as a set of subjects, important though subject matter was, could be adequate for the many demands that would confront the present generations in the next century.

It seemed increasingly likely that a much fuller preparation was necessary, one that involved the development of various personal qualities that would be essential, rather than optional, in future, and one that took into account the teaching and learning strategies that might form an integral, rather than an external and belated, part of the curriculum.

The cubic model is, therefore, a simplified schema of the complexities of the curriculum, offering a series of perspectives on teaching and learning. Like all models it is only as good as those who use it, so I hope no one will do mischief to it. For example, I am at pains to point out (a) that subject matter is very important and this is not diminished by taking a look at other aspects of the curriculum, and (b) that the labels on the cube are only *exemplary*, as many others could have been used. No doubt some skim reader will ignore these warnings. The cubic model does not offer a prescription or a set of solutions, just a means to help reflection and action.

E.C. Wragg,
Exeter University

Acknowledgements

I should like to express my gratitude to the Leverhulme Trust for supporting a number of research projects that I have directed. I should also like to thank the many heads, teachers, advisers and my colleagues in higher education, who usually manage to retain a bit of vision and hope about the future of education, despite the many pressures to concentrate on filling in the forms.

The author and publishers are grateful to the following for permission to reproduce illustrations:

The Greater London Record Office for Figure 3; *Third Age News* for Figure 4; the Science Museum/Science and Society Picture Library for Figure 5; Nelson/Yorkshire International Thomson Multimedia for Figure 6; Longman for Figure 8; Exeter College for Figures 15 and 23; Forbes Publications for Figure 16; Thomas Nelson & Sons Ltd for Figure 22; and *The Times* for permission to use the chess column in Figure 27.

Introducing the Cube

Actually, it isn't a cube. It's a multi-dimensional hyperspace, but *The Multi-dimensional Hyperspace Curriculum* does not exactly have a ring to it. Like all models the cubic curriculum is a simplification of the real world, an attempt to reduce enormous complexity down to something one can try to get inside and explore, while distorting as little as possible in the process. It offers a way of looking at the curriculum from several angles, especially in terms of the subjects being studied, the themes that reach across subjects, and methods of teaching and learning. These related matters can then be considered both separately and in combination.

I shall take the term 'curriculum' to comprise most of what children learn in school, including what is sometimes called the 'hidden curriculum', that is, the values and patterns of behaviour that are acquired, often incidentally – for example, if pupils learn to show concern for others, or to accept authority. I should not want such an elastic definition to be stretched to include absolutely everything that happens within the boundaries of a school, though others might see it this broadly. If the concept of curriculum were to be that vast and comprehensive, then every single private exchange between pupils, whether reprehensible or not, including those that took place out of sight and earshot of teachers, would have to be called part of the 'curriculum'. In this book 'curriculum' includes what is actively sponsored, or else condoned, by the school and its teachers, whether it is labelled on the timetable or not.

There are many ways of considering a school's curriculum along more than one dimension, some of which are described in Chapter 2, and there is no suggestion that what is described here is the sole approach. The cubic curriculum is based on a set of propositions about preparation for what is often regarded as an uncertain future, so it simply offers various ways of looking at life in classrooms along different channels.

FOUR PROPOSITIONS

The argument put forward for the cubic or multi-dimensional view of the curriculum is founded on a number of linked propositions. The first is that *education must incorporate a vision of the future*. Failure to embrace the future would be a cruel deception of millions of young people who are dependent on their elders for much of their education. This does not mean that education should be purely instrumental, based entirely on detailed speculation, possibly wrong-headed, about the needs of citizens in times to come. It involves being aware of the factors likely to affect the lives of those who are in school or college. If you live by a river, then learning to sail a boat might be a useful investment for the future, but 'sailing' should not be the whole curriculum. There is more to human life than boat journeys, and the river might dry up.

The second proposition is that *there are escalating demands on citizens*. In many fields of work and employment there has been what is sometimes called 'spiralling credentialism', the demand for employees to have higher qualifications for jobs than were required from previous generations. In family and home life, people need considerable competence if they are to benefit from a wide range of recreation and leisure opportunities, or avoid being exploited by loan sharks and the many predators who prey on the weak and ill-educated. Being a citizen in the twenty-first century involves knowing your rights and obligations, as well as being able to put your knowledge and skill at the disposal of your fellows. Coping with adult life in the future will require a mixture of personal, social and professional competence.

The third proposition implicit in the cubic curriculum is that, if they are to manage this increasing complexity, *children's learning must be inspired by several influences*. It is unlikely that one aspect of the curriculum alone can achieve all that is necessary. Important though subject matter is, in certain circumstances *how* something is learned may turn out to be as important as *what* is learned. If, when they leave school, pupils recall little from their science lessons, because science was made to seem boring and meaningless, then this sad message may travel with them into their adult life, closing their minds to the miraculous wonders of the world around them.

The fourth and closely related proposition, therefore, is that if life in the future is going to be as demanding and multi-faceted as I describe in Chapter 1 of this book, then *it is essential to see the curriculum as much more than a mere collection of subjects and syllabuses*. The whole of what is experienced in schools and colleges can make an impact on those who attend them. This includes, among other factors, the subject matter being taught; the knowledge, skills, attitudes and patterns of behaviour being learned; the explicit and implicit values and beliefs in education; the forms of teaching and learning which are employed. There are many angles and dimensions to be considered.

THE CUBIC CURRICULUM

A cube is a perfect three-dimensional model, where each side is exactly the same length. The model I describe in Chapter 2 onwards of this book is three-dimensional, but there could be four, five or more dimensions, what is called 'hyperspace'. Each side in the model could be the same size, but each might also be different from the rest. In other words, the cuboid shape in this particular model is a rough approximation. *It is illustrative, rather than exact*. It is meant to open up understanding and debate, rather than close them down. *The labels in Figure 1 are not meant to represent, or advocate a particular curriculum, therefore.* They are there as examples of the sort of subjects, themes, or teaching and learning strategies that might be present in a school or college.

The three principal dimensions of the cube in Figure 1 are (1) the subjects being taught, such as mathematics, or music, (2) cross-curricular themes and issues that influence children's general development, like 'language' or 'thought', and (3) the forms of teaching and learning which are employed, such as 'telling' or 'discovering'.

Consider two entirely fictitious children. Child A spends every day of her childhood alone in the same room with the same teacher. She is never allowed to speak, only to listen. She is only taught history, no other subject. When she is 18 she is told to go out into the world and join the rest of society. Meanwhile Child B studies several subjects with many different teachers. He listens to his teachers, but he is also encouraged to speak about what he is learning both with teachers and with other pupils, do practical work, investigate and explore the world around him. When he is 18 he too is told to go out into the world.

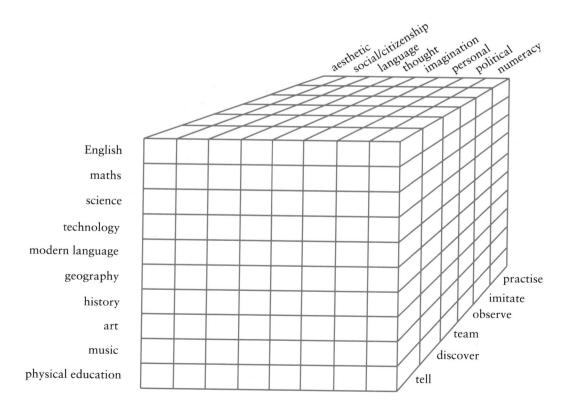

Figure 1   The cubic curriculum

In terms of the cubic curriculum, Child A has operated almost entirely in one channel of the first dimension, as she has studied only one subject, history, though this may have included the history of science or mathematics and touched on other disciplines. In the second dimension she may have studied a number of themes, but only in the context of history. When it comes to the third dimension, here too she has operated principally in one mode, that of being told. Her curriculum is intense and may not be entirely without merit, but in terms of what is possible for children she has had a very narrow diet.

Child B has operated down several channels of the first dimension of the cubic curriculum, having studied a number of subjects. He may well have derived benefit from many cross-curricular themes in the second dimension, as his language and thought, for example, develop in different contexts. In the third dimension he will have also experienced more than one form of learning, sometimes being told, on other occasions finding out for himself or working closely with others. Since he, like Child A, is fictitious, he may, for all one knows, have spread his efforts so thinly that he has become master of nothing, or he may equally have become just the sort of well-rounded 'whole person' that government curriculum documents have been seeking for years.

The cubic curriculum is a model which can be used in many different ways. The three major dimensions can be studied separately or together. Parts of the cube can be considered for specific purposes. For example, someone might want to know how children's thinking is being developed in different subjects, so there could be particular scrutiny of the 'thought' channel in the second dimension. Each individual cell in the cube can be looked at, so when a teacher gives someone a piece of information about a technical term used in science, like 'gravity' or 'mammal', then this transaction takes place in the 'science–language/thought–tell' parts of the cube.

The model allows not only teachers, pupils or anyone else interested to study individual children's experiences of schooling along various dimensions, it also permits scrutiny of the whole school, or indeed of the whole national effort. As will be shown in Chapter 6, a teacher or other observer can follow a class around for a period of time to see what life is like across different subjects, topics and activities for whole classes, groups or individuals.

On a much larger scale, a whole nation could review what is happening in its schools. In a number of countries, often with high educational standards like Japan, there has been a concern about whether children, knowledgeable though they may be when they leave school, have developed enough 'individualism'. If in the third dimension of the cubic curriculum, the forms of teaching and learning, there has been a concentration in schools almost entirely on the transmission mode, 'telling', then it would not be surprising if opportunities for the development of individualism had been eclipsed.

THE CONTENTS OF THE BOOK

The beliefs lying behind this book are based on the four propositions given above, namely that (1) we must try to have a vision of the future, even if it appears complex; (2) so far as we can see the future will demand a great deal from the young people facing it; (3) a fuller vision of the curriculum is necessary, as children should be subject to several influences, not just one, and; (4) if the curriculum is to be seen as more than a set of subjects, each with a syllabus, the multi-dimensional view being put forward here, albeit in simplified cubic form, might help in the planning of a richer experience of schooling for both teachers and learners.

Chapter 1 describes a complex and speculative vision of a future in which children now in school will require considerable competence if they are to prosper. If the twenty-first century follows the trends I describe, then citizens will need a mixture of knowledge and skills, as well as personal qualities like determination, flexibility and imagination. In Chapter 2 the cubic curriculum is explained in more detail, in an attempt to show how a multi-dimensional view of schooling is necessary in order to prepare for the rapidly changing and demanding world that young adults will enter.

Chapters 3, 4 and 5 describe the three major dimensions of the cubic curriculum. The first dimension, the very important matter of the subjects that are studied in schools and colleges, is covered in Chapter 3. The second dimension, the cross-curricular themes and issues, is dealt with in Chapter 4. The third dimension, the forms of teaching and learning, is omitted from many discussions about curriculum, though in other cases it is carefully integrated with subject and thematic concerns. These issues are addressed in Chapter 5. None of this would be of any interest, however, if it did not lead to more effective teaching and learning, so in Chapter 6, I attempt to show how the whole model can be brought together to analyse, and hopefully improve, what is happening in the classroom.

I have aimed this book at a varied readership, not only for professionals working in the field, but also for the thousands of others who have an interest or direct stake in education. I have tried, wherever possible therefore, to avoid the sort of jargon that puts people off grappling with key educational issues. Where I give examples from my own or other people's research projects, I have attempted to use straightforward language, to give the essence of what has been discovered without doing mischief to the findings.

It is sometimes asserted that schooling can have relatively little influence on people, since, allowing for holidays and weekends, children may only spend on average about 25 hours a week in the company of their teachers. This is about the same amount of time as the average child devotes to watching television. Yet almost all adults can recall vividly a number of critical events that occurred in their own schooldays. It is not easy to prove a direct causal link between what happens in classrooms and what people eventually do or believe in their adult lives. However, if we believed that nothing that happened in school had any effect, we might as well close schools down. My own belief is that there is a great deal to play for. That is why it is important to create the most effective and impact-making curriculum, in the full sense of the word 'curricu-lum', that we possibly can.

Education is our investment in the future. Were the future full of certainties, then planning a curriculum might be more straightforward. Life in the twenty-first century, in which children now in school will spend their adult years, is difficult to predict. Yet we need to have at least a speculative vision of the future on which to base some of our thinking and action about the curriculum. Conjecture about what is in store for young people is bound to be imperfect and problematic, so I shall address that first.

CHAPTER ONE

Life in the Future

Some of the children in school today may see the dawn of the twenty-second century. With improved medical treatments being devised every day, there is a strong likelihood that children born in the late twentieth and early twenty-first centuries will, in many cases, live to be 90, 100, or more. In these circumstances the term 'future' can mean a very long time indeed. If education is society's investment in its own posterity, then a long- rather than a short-term strategy is essential.

It is easy to argue that education must be based on a vision of the future, but not so simple to describe what that future might look like. There have been numerous predictions about life in the twenty-first century, some gloomy, others more hopeful. Indeed, the same data can be quoted to support either a pessimistic or optimistic vision of what is to come. Forecasts that job opportunities may diminish can be used to predict boredom and street riots, or to welcome the release of people from dangerous and demeaning employment.

Speculation about the future involves intelligent guesswork about present and past trends and where they might eventually lead, so that key messages about the twenty-first century can be elicited. Predictions can, of course, go disastrously astray, which is why they should be read with caution. It would be a mistake to base a whole education system entirely on a single conjecture, especially when it is hazardous enough predicting next year's events on the basis of what is happening this year. Small wonder that the great oracles have often spoken in ambiguous terms. I propose to deal here, therefore, with a range of possibilities that seem to be worth considering, and see what the implications would be were they to materialise, though none of the following messages is offered with any certainty.

EMPLOYMENT OR UNEMPLOYMENT?

While the jobs that people hold do not consume the whole of their life, they are an important part of it. In the first half of the twentieth century many men, if they lived long enough, worked for some 50 or so years before entering retirement, while women tended to work in paid employment for fewer years, or did not return to their previous career after giving birth to children. Speculations about the future often concentrate entirely on the nature of employment or the lack of it. What is clear is that changes in work patterns have been dramatic in the last third of the twentieth century. What is less clear is where these changes are leading.

During the nineteenth century a succession of industrial revolutions saw masses of people move out of the rural areas and into the cities, as they left agriculture to seek work in factories. Whereas in early Victorian Britain about a third of the population worked on the land, the figure in modern times is of about 2 per cent of the workforce employed in agriculture, a remarkable transformation in the landscape of working life. Equally significant changes took place during the last three decades of the twentieth century, but the eventual outcome of these post-industrial revolutions remains clouded. The massive disappearance of jobs in manufacturing industry has not led to a single type of employer emerging to absorb those displaced during the labour-shedding process.

During the 1970s in the United Kingdom, over a million jobs were lost in manufacturing industry alone. Another one and a half million went in the first five years of the 1980s. The turmoil continued towards the end of the century, and in the first five years of the 1990s some 5 million people lost their job. What was notable about these huge losses of traditional forms of employment was first of all that the vast majority of posts that disappeared were unskilled, semi-skilled or barely skilled. It is true that graduate employment also suffered, but the biggest decline was in areas where machines were brought in to perform the numerous tasks that had previously been carried out by armies of worker ants. Firms that used to employ dozens of girl school-leavers to fill cardboard boxes with their products, and dozens of boy school-leavers to load them on to lorries, replaced the girls with automated packing machines and the boys with a couple of fork-lift truck operators. For those without skill the prospects became bleak.

Another aspect of higher unemployment was that it appeared to be endemic rather than cyclical. Recessions earlier in the century had been followed by boom times. The order books emptied, but then filled up again, as world or national trading prospects improved. Workers dropped to a three-day week, or lost their jobs, only to regain exactly the same posts later, often with bonus and overtime payments, as the economy moved into a higher gear. When the cycle stopped it was partly because, in the new automated economy, no employer was going to get rid of two fork-lift trucks and two drivers in order to employ 20 people with large biceps.

There also appeared to be a paradox, in that, even in areas of high unemployment, there were vacancies. Unfortunately the vacancies did not always match the talents and skills of the jobless. It was of little consolation to the dispossessed coal miner or steel worker to see a job advert asking for someone to repair video recorders or computers. This meant that retraining became an important matter. Those who either had no skills to sell, or whose skills had become outmoded, needed to acquire fresh knowledge and skills in order to become employable again. There were sad examples of people who did retrain and then managed to obtain another post, only to experience redundancy in their newly found career. For some people serial retraining was in itself to become a significant feature of their lives.

Figure 2 The fork-lift truck – obliterated many unskilled jobs

Nor was retraining confined to the unskilled or those who worked in traditional craft trades in manufacturing industry. Secretaries had to acquire the skills of word processing and other forms of information technology. Surgeons had to learn transplant surgery, the use of immuno-suppressive drugs, laser technology. Head teachers were pressed to turn into financial, marketing and resource-management experts. Trade-union officials, previously regarded as wage negotiators, found themselves increasingly involved in advising their workmates about compensation for accidents, or the workings of an industrial tribunal for those who had lost their jobs. As well as the oral competence that had always been necessary to fulfil their duties, they needed higher reading competence in order to cope with the literature on health and safety at work, or employment protection. Some forms of knowledge and skill seemed to have a very short life before becoming obsolete. Few employees escaped the remorseless march of novelty and innovation.

In addition to these kinds of change there were new working patterns for the many still in work. The development of new technology meant that certain kinds of activity could be done at least as well, and sometimes at lower cost, in the home, or in a remote satellite location at a distance from the main centre of production. Publishing, journalism, garment manufacture, design work, telephone sales, consultancy and advice, many of these could, given the right equipment, be carried out as easily in someone's attic, as in a noisy and crowded office or factory. There was also a shift to much more part-time employment, and women in particular often took jobs that required part of the day, rather than the whole of it. Many people moved to part-time employment as an element of an early retirement package. Hutton (1995) estimated the number of British part-time workers in the late twentieth century to be in excess of 5 million, of whom 80 per cent were women.

At its best this meant that some degree of control over time was returned to the individual. Instead of having to leave home in the early morning to ensure arrival at the start of the working day, only to have to battle against traffic once more in the evening, those with flexible working arrangements could sometimes suit themselves. The shift to part-time working and phased retirement liberated parts of the day and week for recreation or leisure, or for more time with family and friends.

At its worst, however, part-timers and home workers were exploited, paid low wages, denied the same safety and employment protection rights as full-timers. Since some 70 per cent of all new part-time jobs were for 16 hours a week or less (Hutton, 1995), this meant that the holders of them had no right to appeal against unfair dismissal or to redundancy payments. Much time had to be expended, by those who would have preferred a full-time post, trying to stitch together several part-time jobs. There were numerous examples of families dropping to a lower standard of living, because the male adult had lost his full-time job and the female adult had only been able to obtain a part-time post.

As traditional jobs disappeared in the manufacturing sector, so new ones began to appear in service and support industries. Alongside smaller numbers of the big employers of labour, there sprang up numerous small and medium-sized businesses. Unfortunately a number of these did not succeed, and bankruptcies increased as several small concerns ceased training. This added to the problems of those seeking work, as small firms closed and some failed entrepreneurs returned to being employees of someone else.

The messages about employment prospects in the twenty-first century from this rapidly changing environment are mixed, but some possibilities emerge that need to be considered by those working in education. They include the following, all of which might continue into the future along similar trend lines.

- The numbers of unskilled and semi-skilled jobs appear to be in considerable decline, therefore a *much higher level of knowledge and skill* will be necessary from those wishing to enter, or remain in employment.
- More jobs in service and support, leisure and recreation, rather than in factories, means that *social skills*, the ability to get on with others, may become more valued.

- People may have to retrain significantly several times in their adult lives, perhaps every five to seven years, so *flexibility* and *willingness to continue learning* are important.
- As more people take part-time jobs, or work from their own home or in a place remote from their employer's headquarters, qualities such as *independence*, *resourcefulness* and *adaptability* may be highly valued.
- People will need to know their rights and entitlements, as well as their obligations to others, if they are to play a full part in society and not be exploited by the unscrupulous.

HOME AND FAMILY LIFE

It is not yet entirely clear whether a reduction in the time spent at work will in practice lead to more time being available for home and family life. This is partly because of a paradox. Although the number of unemployed has increased since the 1950s and 1960s, those who have full-time jobs often worker longer hours than they did in earlier times. Some people have too little to do, while others have too much.

The increase in working hours is explained by a number of factors. It is partly because of what Handy (1994) called the '$\frac{1}{2} \times 2 \times 3$' formula – from a company's point of view, productivity and profit could be increased if half the previous workforce were paid twice their salary to obtain three times as much output. Another explanation is the increased commuting time, as employees travel greater distances to seek work, without wanting to move house as well. A further reason is the tendency, during a recession, for people to take on additional evening or weekend jobs, or to pursue income-generating 'hobbies', like vegetable growing, collecting (buying and selling artefacts), decorating or car repair.

Uncertainties in the workplace can lead to insecurity in home and family life. Part-time workers, as well as those likely to lose or have to change their job, are less able to secure the sort of mortgage that will purchase a good-quality home. Those working long hours may have less time and energy left over for family and social life. Some factors appear to have combined to reduce the time spent on physical activity. The degree of strenuous exercise necessary to reduce the incidence of heart disease is thought to be three periods of 20 minutes per week in which the heart rate rises to more than 140 beats a minute. Relatively few adults reach this level, as do few children. The availability of considerable opportunities for spectator entertainment, such as watching multi-channel television or attending sports events, may prevent many adults from being more physically active.

Even in home and family life greater knowledge and skill appear to be necessary than in former times. Families may run into considerable debt if they are unable to manage their own finances. In desperation some may fall victim to 'loan sharks' and others who prey on the ill-educated, paying vast amounts of interest on small loans which leave them in thrall for years. The predators in society exploit those whose rudimentary levels of numeracy, literacy or oral competence mean they are unable to calculate percentages, read legalistic agreements, or argue with articulate and persuasive usurers. In our complex bureaucratic society those unable to compose a letter, attend and speak at a public meeting, or combine with others to lobby decision makers, may find their child is unable to obtain the school place of their choice, or that a six-lane highway is to be driven through their back garden.

Recreation and leisure require knowledge and skill. It is quite true that those with little knowledge and skill can still enjoy their leisure, but their choices may be fewer. Under the 'minimal competency testing' programme run in several parts of the United States, one paper on 'life skills' was partly based on the guide to Yosemite National Park. The minimal competency tests were an attempt to identify those who might quit their schooling with only rudimentary competence, ill-equipped to face life in the twenty-first century. Responses to this paper on 'life skills' showed that some pupils were unable to read the guide well enough to understand what there was to be enjoyed.

Inability to read proficiently, understand map signs and conventions, calculate the time and cost of taking a family on an outing, do not prevent people from visiting Yosemite, but the less competent do have more limited opportunities than the competent, in recreation as in work. When the working week is reduced, some people fill it up again with 'leisure' activities that are not unlike what would be 'work' for others, hence the popularity of 'do-it-yourself' stores, as well as pastimes such as gardening, decorating, cookery and car maintenance. Many of these hobbies and pastimes require the same or similar knowledge and skills as would be needed for someone in paid employment, like understanding how electricity works, the ability to use a power tool, read instructions, or work harmoniously alongside others.

This last point is also an important one more generally, and relates to a number of messages for education for the future which emerge from looking at home and family life.

- In the twenty-first century, especially if the working week were to be reduced, or more people worked in their own house or flat, extra time would be available away from the workplace to be spent in the home or community; some would use these additional hours for work-like activities, others for leisure.
- There may be a trend towards less personal physical activity and more spectating, with possible consequences for individual health.
- In home and family life, the ability to get on well with one's fellows is an important quality, if breakdowns in relationships are to be avoided.
- Consideration of both working and social life in the future suggests that the needs for both domains may be similar, if not identical.
- Wide rather than rudimentary knowledge, a broad range of skills, the ability to relate well to others, personal qualities and traits, such as imagination, determination, flexibility, a willingness to learn throughout one's life, are important prerequisites for all aspects of adult life.

THE FOUR AGES

One of the most notable trends during the twentieth century was the changes in what are sometimes called the Four Ages. The First Age is the age of full-time education and training, the Second Age the period of working life, the Third Age the years of healthy retirement, and the Fourth Age represents the time of infirmity. Since the nineteenth century, when large numbers of people never even reached the later ages, the transformation has been dramatic. Children in school today, for example, may find that it is their Third, rather than their Second Age, which occupies the greatest number of years.

Furthermore, the Four Ages may become increasingly fluid and ill defined, flowing and fusing into each other, as many people stay in education, while others enter work, or some retire early, while their contemporaries work on. In the twenty-first century one 45-year-old may wish to take up a new job and therefore commence a significant programme of retraining, possibly on a full-time basis, effectively returning to the state of dependency of the First Age. Another 45-year-old may be contemplating starting a lengthy period of part-time employment between the ages of 45 and 70, dropping first to a four-day week, then to half-time, and eventually to one day a week, blurring the boundaries between the Second and Third Ages. A third 45-year-old may be finishing work entirely, entering the Third Age two or three decades ahead of other contemporaries. Yet another person of the same age may never have held a job at all, and therefore effectively have skipped from the First to the Third Age, without a Second Age in between.

Each of the Four Ages has transformed dramatically since the last century. The First Age has tended to become longer in recent times. For much of the nineteenth century children were not required to attend school at all, and in many cases commenced employment at the age of 10 or earlier. The twentieth century saw a significant lengthening of the First Age as, in the United Kingdom, the school-leaving age was fixed at 14 following the First World War, at 15 after the Second World War, and at 16 in the 1970s. Subsequently, the advent of higher unemployment produced a variety of youth training schemes, first of a few months and later lasting one and eventually two years. This effectively lengthened the First Age from less than a decade in the nineteenth century, to more like 18 years for the majority by the late twentieth century.

During this period there was another important change. Evidence from earlier in the nineteenth century shows that girls, on average, entered the age of menarche – that is, started their periods – at about the age of 17. By the late twentieth century the average age of menarche was down to about $12\frac{1}{2}$. Boys tend to start their adolescent growth spurt a year or 18 months later than girls, so this meant that most children were reaching physical adulthood at around the age of 14 rather than at about 18.

Whereas in the nineteenth century children left the First Age physically immature and were still children for the first few years of their Second Age, when they commenced work, by the late twentieth century it was the exact opposite. They reached physical maturity, only to find that they had to spend at least four, and possibly up to ten more years in the First Age, unable to start in a job. Given that boys in particular often go through a period of aggression on reaching physical maturity, secondary schools found that they had to contain and educate potentially aggressive young adults who, 100 years previously, would have been well into their Second Age and off school premises. What had been an external social problem in Victorian times had now become an internal school problem. The school-leaving age cannot rise indefinitely, nor can the onset of adolescence fall continually, but a longer First Age looks likely to be a feature of the twenty-first century, when it might become 20 years or more for the majority.

As the First Age has lengthened, so the Second Age has shortened, and at both ends. Children entered work later, and adults began to leave it earlier. For many in Victorian times the Second Age was virtually their whole life, as killer diseases like typhoid and tuberculosis, the ravages of war, and deaths in childbirth robbed millions of their Third and Fourth Age. The age of retirement came down to 70 and later to 65, but then it moved lower still during the late twentieth century, as more and more opted for early or phased retirement, or simply lost their jobs and had to take enforced leave from paid employment. Fifty years and a gold watch gave way to 40 years or less, followed by a part-time post for the more fortunate. It is difficult to say what the

Figure 3   A rudimentary education during a short First Age, 1908, Whitechapel
Courtesy of Greater London Record Office, Photograph Collection

Second Age will become in future for those currently in school, as it may be that improved health in later years might lead to its lengthening once more, if people choose and have opportunities to work into their seventies. Present indications are that for many people it may not last more than 35 years.

In stark contrast, the Third Age, the period of healthy retirement that was non-existent for most in the nineteenth century, when a mere 6 or so per cent of the population was over 60, is becoming dramatically longer, as the 60-plus age group swells to a quarter or more of the population. Handy (1994) cites surveys showing that only a third of British adults over the age of 55 are still in paid employment, and in France and Italy the figures are 27 per cent and 11 per cent respectively. Many children currently in school may, therefore, experience 20, 30 or even 40 years in the Third Age. This particular social change has considerable implications for education, since children who are disenchanted with their schooling may be reluctant to take on fresh intellectual challenges in their Third Age.

The evidence suggests that older people are perfectly capable of learning new knowledge and skills. Although they may need a little more time and slightly longer intervals between 'lessons', they can often draw on a wider range of strategies than are available to younger people with more limited experience. Indeed the 'University of the Third Age' is an institution that caters for those who, in retirement, wish to use their knowledge and experience to teach one another. The Open University has thousands

Figure 4   Eighty-year-old Joanne Walker receives her certificate for 'outstanding performance in computer literacy', University of the Third Age, Darlington Branch
Source: *Third Age News*, Autumn 1996

of students who go on to graduate in their seventies and eighties. Even during the Fourth Age, the time of infirmity, when the elderly may be confined indoors, most will be perfectly capable of continuing to learn something new, and continued mental activity in old age is often closely associated with better general health.

The story of centenarian Charles Warrell is interesting here. A retired teacher who lived to be 106, he became well known as the author of the *Big Chief I-spy* books and newspaper columns which sold over 40 million copies. At the age of 92 Charles bought an old oak chest. He tried to find out when it had been made, but without success initially, so he went to the library, sent away for furniture books, and eventually, after much assiduous research, managed to track down its origins. A year later, aged 93, he then wrote an article about the chest which was published in a national magazine. When he was 104 he was still telephoning friends to find out about recent developments in schools. It may be exceptional today for someone to develop and pursue with determination a fresh interest in his nineties, and to be still interested in his former profession after reaching the age of 100, but this may be a commonplace in the later twenty-first century for those currently in school. Already, according to 1990 census data, there are more than 36,000 centenarians living in the United States. Hence the importance for the highly significant Third Age, and the not insignificant Fourth Age, of effective groundwork, particularly during the First Age.

The messages for education from these massive changes in the Four Ages are clear:

- The longer First Age, with its more extended period of education, lays down foundations for what could be another 70 years or more of active learning; it is vital, therefore, that this first phase is well conceived and regarded as a positive experience.
- The Second Age, though shorter than in previous generations, is none the less a time when continued learning and the flexibility to adapt are likely to be extremely important, both in work and recreation.
- The Third Age may for many people be the longest of the Four Ages, a time when they may have the time to take on significant new interests, making it even more important to lay firm foundations on which to build during the First and Second Ages.
- Even those who are housebound in the Fourth Age will want to continue to be mentally active and this can be beneficial for a longer and healthier life.
- The boundaries between the Four Ages may well become much more diffuse, and individuals will enter and pass through them at different times, in different ways and at different speeds.

THE KNOWLEDGE EXPLOSION

It is several centuries since the 'Universal Man' was thought to be capable of grasping all the knowledge available to the world at the time, and it was dubious then whether anyone could really absorb all of what was known. In the eighteenth century writers like Goethe, who composed poetry, novels, plays, historical and philosophical works, and even a scientific treatise, were admired as complete scholars. Yet even at that time they only knew a fraction of what had been discovered.

Today the quest for universal knowledge would be an impossibility, as millions of books, articles, films, radio and television programmes, as well as ideas expressed in electronic media, are produced every year. Even with access to international databases containing millions of research findings in every field, it is inconceivable that anyone will personally know more than the tiniest portion of all knowledge available in their discipline or area of interest. It is both impossible and undesirable to halt the gathering of knowledge; it seems to be an activity which will, if anything, continue to quicken in future.

The consequences for education of this remorseless addition to the store of human knowledge are of several kinds. First of all, though we cannot know everything, we have to know something. Hence the interminable debates and discussions about the *content* of various subject curricula. In a vast field like health education, for example, what should children study at the age of 5, 8, 11 or 14? When can they best learn about dental care, the need for a healthy diet and exercise regime, or the effects on health of smoking, alcohol or drugs? What information, skills, attitudes and forms of behaviour might they need to acquire? When might be too late and when too soon to study a particular topic? These questions will be discussed further in Chapter 3, for they lie right at the heart of the first dimension of the cubic curriculum, the subjects being learned.

The second consequence of the knowledge explosion is that if we cannot learn everything in school, and have to settle for a small proportion of what exists, then we have to know how to *find out* for ourselves. The ability to track down vital information, abstract its essence, work out how to apply what we have learned, often without external help, is a key element of independence of mind and action. Most adults have to make numerous decisions on their own during the day, some trivial, like where to shop, others more profound, like what actions to take in their working or home life. This ability to explore, discover and then act, often with tenacity and imagination, is particularly crucial given the points made earlier about the length of adult life and the importance of the Third Age. It is also an important element of the second and third dimensions of the cubic curriculum, the cross-curricular themes and forms of teaching and learning, as people will need to acquire these crucial transferable skills at an early stage if they are to be autonomous in adult life.

The third major consequence of exponential growth in knowledge gathering is that if we can neither know nor find out everything, then we will probably need to *work with others*, in order to amplify and enhance our individual efforts. While it is true that a committee would not have painted the Mona Lisa, or composed Beethoven's Fifth Symphony, it is also the case that no individual could have sent a manned spacecraft to the moon. The advantage of working in a team is that, if it is successful, its collective effort should exceed the sum of what its individual members might have achieved.

The United States government agency NASA (National Aeronautics and Space

Administration) is able to employ some of the world's leading authorities on the calculation of rocket flight paths, the materials out of which spacecraft are made, rocket fuels, diet during space flights, the fabrics of astronauts' clothing, the psychology of being in space, medical aspects of space travel and a host of other topics. If a space mission has an accident and goes astray, it is rescued not by one heroic individual, but by a huge team of experts working in collaboration. In the twenty-first century major social, as well as technological and scientific problems are likely to be resolved by small or large teams.

The ability and willingness to make one's knowledge and skill available to others will be a major contribution to many successes in the future, and this has relevance for all three of the cubic curriculum dimensions. Developing a high level of expertise in a particular field is a prerequisite for being in a position to offer knowledge and skill in the first place, and the specialist field may become more and more narrow as more and more is discovered within its domain.

This is an issue of vital importance to the first dimension of the cubic curriculum. If expertise tends to narrow, then developing interests and understanding beyond the confines of one's specialism is also important, and this is germane to the second dimension, the cross-curricular. Nurturing the ability to collaborate with others is the next vital step, and this notion is central to the third dimension of the cubic

Figure 5   NASA at work
Courtesy: Science Museum/Science and Society Picture Library

curriculum, for the ways in which children learn and are taught may transmit significant messages about how they should conduct themselves in their adult life.

The messages being emitted from analysis of the continuing rapid growth of knowledge, therefore, are manifold, but they include the following:

- Since pupils cannot learn everything, thought must be given to what might best be learned at different stages of their development.
- Not being able to learn everything means that the ability and willingness to find out for oneself is an important prerequisite for lifelong autonomy.
- Major social, technological and scientific problems will be solved by smaller or larger teams of players, each member being highly knowledgeable and skilled, but also able and willing to make expertise available to others.
- As knowledge expands, fields of expertise may continue to narrow, and this has significance for each of the dimensions of the cubic curriculum.

NEW TECHNOLOGY AND LEARNING

The development of any new form of technological aid in education is usually over-hyped by its developer. It will, the public is told, revolutionise teaching, allow all those who have failed by other means to reach genius level in a short time, and probably replace the need for having a teacher at all. The truth, alas, is often more mundane, as the latest miracle takes its place in history alongside all the other pieces of machinery that added to the learning opportunities available, but did not solve every problem.

The development of radio as a teaching tool in the 1920s, and the advent of slide projectors, film, television, tape recorders, teaching machines, all these were hailed as the ultimate solution to numerous problems: ending the shortages of qualified teachers, catering for the difficulties faced by children in remote areas, providing work exactly matched to the needs of the individual learner. Each did indeed perform a useful service and, sometimes in modified form, has found a niche in the repertoire of many teachers. Subsequent technological developments may pass through a similar cycle: over-hype by developers – adoption by enthusiasts – spread to a wider constituency of practitioners – assumption of a modest, or more significant place in the mainstream of teaching aids.

What characterised the forms of new technology developed in the last few years of the twentieth century was (1) huge memory, (2) the opportunities for interaction, and (3) the use of several kinds of media – print, graphics, voice, music, animation, still and moving photographic pictures – alone or in combination. The micro-computer, CD ROMs, adapted games machines, 'virtual reality' and the 'information superhighway' as it was sometimes called, all these offered more opportunities for interaction, for the learner to interrogate and probe, than did earlier, more passive forms of educational technology.

While studying a topic like 'the structure of the atom', people might watch a video, or listen to a tape, but when using interactive technology, they are able to ask questions, albeit often in limited form. Pupils using a video or sound tape about atomic structure have to be fairly passive, as the programme maker has decided what information shall be transmitted and in what form. The same pupils using a CD ROM, or other form of interactive technology, could look at a model of an atom, add to it or subtract from it, rotate it, and at the same time learn the consequences of what they have done. For example, the periodic table might be displayed on their screen and they might be told that what started off as a hydrogen atom has now become an atom of helium. It is as if they have their own set of coloured components and an individual teacher to tell them after every move what they have just done. Moreover, the memory power of the machine allows every key stroke to be recorded and profiles of progress to be assembled at the press of a button.

The history of some new technology is that it began its life principally as a leisure or games machine which then became used for educational purposes. The exceptionally powerful memories of certain games machines were especially suited to education,

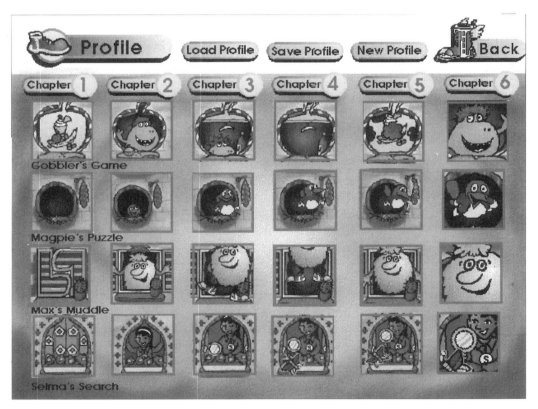

Figure 6   CD-ROM profile of children learning to read. The teacher can check the child's performance on each of the activities
Source: *Flying Boot* CD-ROM, Nelson Yorkshire International Thomson Multimedia, Teacher's Guide for the Maximania CD-ROM

offering many opportunities to combine film, still picture, animation, sound and written text. 'Virtual reality', originally regarded in the popular mind as a games helmet, worn over the head by those who wanted to pretend they were up in space zapping invading aliens, soon became used to train surgeons or to explore environments that children might not be able to visit normally, like the rain forests or the moon.

The information superhighway, the fibre-optic communications network of finely spun, hair-like slivers of glass that could carry film, sound, music, graphics and text to every home and institution in the country, was also heralded as another great educational breakthrough that might one day remove the need for teachers. However, the presence, in multi-media form, of immense amounts of information, is no guarantee at all that learning will take place.

Information is not the same as knowledge. Information is 'out there'; knowledge is what is inside the brain, digested and understood. Indeed, children in particular, unable to chart a path through the dense mass, might despair if left to explore unaided. What is essential in this burgeoning expanse of information is people who can structure and track what is going on, in other words *annotators* who can help to unravel and explain what might otherwise be an enormous bewildering maze. Possible annotators include not only teachers, but also writers, publishers, broadcasters. In the future, as in the present, numerous sources of information will be available to pupils other than what their teachers choose to bring before them, and it will be important for them to develop the skill and resourcefulness not only to act on advice and help, but also to pursue their own pathways through what they are studying.

The messages about the use of current and as yet unimagined new technology include the following:

- People will be even more liberated than they are at present from dependence on a teacher as the single source of knowledge.
- Learning in remote locations, with or without others, will become easier, so the ability to learn autonomously will be important.
- The huge memory and the highly interactive nature of many of the newer forms of educational technology permit many different forms of teaching and learning.
- Information is not the same as knowledge, and so annotators, like teachers, writers and broadcasters, are important agents for ensuring that complex and diverse information is properly understood.

A CURRICULUM FOR THE FUTURE

Many of the speculations and guesses in this chapter are interlinked. If both work and home life really do become more complex and require more knowledge and skill, then citizens of the twenty-first century will require far more competence than the simple notion of 'basics' put forward by some politicians. The modest ability to 'read, write and add up', proposed by British Prime Minister John Major at his party conference in 1994, is far too rudimentary for the demands of the future. The disappearance of millions of unskilled jobs, and the pressures and stresses faced by many quite ordinary people in their daily lives, combine to increase substantially the entry fee into our society for young adults in the twenty-first century.

If many of the children now in school have to retrain several times during their working lives, and if most of them can look forward to many years of good health in their Third Age, then their appetite for learning must stretch way beyond the years of compulsory schooling. In order to flourish over what could be a very long lifetime, they will need a firm foundation of knowledge, skills, attitudes and forms of behaviour, alongside positive personal characteristics, such as determination, flexibility, imagination. They will also require the social intelligence and will to pool their strengths with those of their fellows, as well as the independence of mind to act autonomously. This strong combination of personal and intellectual qualities is particularly important, given the massive explosion of knowledge, which continues to gather pace. The many forms of new interactive technology available require vision and tenacity from those wishing to benefit from them, if they are to be used to their full potential.

In the circumstances, a single dimension view of the curriculum would be inadequate. It is simply not enough to conceive of a school or college curriculum as nothing more than a flat, unidimensional list of subjects or topics. In order to develop the range of talents needed for a prosperous future, children must learn over a wide range and in a variety of ways. That is why a multi-dimensional view of the curriculum makes good sense. The most significant and exciting challenge facing the whole of society, not just those who work professionally in education, is how to devise and provide a coherent programme for young people that recognises the many forces at work, anticipating successfully some of the needs of an uncertain future, synthesising the distilled wisdom of hundreds of generations, while at the same time sponsoring both autonomy and teamwork.

If this can be done successfully, then teachers can actually help their pupils to shape the future, rather than find themselves the unwitting and impotent victims of it. The role of .driver can be much more attractive than that of passenger. The cubic curriculum described in the rest of this book attempts to address the many demands along different channels in three key dimensions. It is to the detail of these that I shall now turn.

CHAPTER TWO

The Cubic Curriculum

A MULTI-DIMENSIONAL CURRICULUM

There is sometimes a belief that, if a country has a legally required National Curriculum, the need for teachers and others to analyse and reflect on curricular matters has disappeared. This is a dreary and unnecessarily restrictive view which would inhibit teachers' professionalism if taken literally. There are, of course, significant differences in practice in different countries, so the opportunities to determine what happens in the classroom will be greater in some cases than in others. In the United States there is no National Curriculum, but individual school district and state requirements may influence what is taught. In countries like England, France or Norway, there is a National Curriculum, with varying degrees of flexibility for decisions to be taken at school or local level about how it should be implemented.

There may be less room for manoeuvre in some countries compared with the greater freedom available in others, but even if a National Curriculum is fairly restrictive, there are still usually opportunities for significant decision making, by teachers and pupils, since it is impossible for somebody outside the school to prescribe every conceivable micro-strategy on a day-to-day basis. One important element of the craft skills of teaching, therefore, is the ability to pick ways through a curriculum, even a prescribed one, via as imaginative and challenging routes as possible.

So far I have argued that, if we are preparing children for a diverse and complex future, then it is simply not enough to think of their curriculum as being merely a set of subjects, each with a syllabus. I am putting forward what I hope is a deeper vision than this, the difference between the 'flat Earth' view of our planet and the three-dimensional globe. There are many examples of this fuller view of schooling, both in theoretical and practical form. These can be found in the literature on curriculum and also built into a number of curriculum packages on different subjects for various age groups.

One way of deepening the analysis of what children are learning is to look across the whole curriculum at certain overarching issues. The philosopher Hirst (1974) put forward the proposition that human beings have developed a rational way of making sense of the world they experience through what he called 'forms of knowledge'. Each of these has its own unique concepts and methods of testing its beliefs, so that teachers' and pupils' approach to analysing religious convictions, for example, would not be exactly the same as the methods they used for testing scientific hypotheses. Other writers like Stenhouse (1975) and Dearden (1976) have also stated their own version of forms of knowledge. Stenhouse argued that the curriculum should be based on some of the principles of enquiry and thought that these forms of knowledge required.

Some of this thinking was influential on the proposals by Her Majesty's Inspectorate (1977) about what they called 'areas of learning and experience'. Originally they put forward eight such areas, but then modified these later (HMI, 1985) to nine. Wilcox and Eustace (1980) used the original eight areas of experience postulated by Her Majesty's Inspectorate in 1977 to draw up a two-dimensional curriculum analysis. Teachers of different subjects were asked to assign a number of points out of 10 to indicate the extent to which they felt their own subject was contributing to each of the eight areas of experience, which included notions such as 'aesthetic and creative', 'scientific' and 'spiritual'. They were then able to add up the points assigned to particular areas of experience in the various subjects taught in the school, and thus see from the profile obtained how much emphasis appeared to be given to each of the eight.

In an interesting project on primary education, Ashton *et al.* (1975) used a similar approach, this time to focus on teachers' aims. They devised a two-dimensional grid which allowed teachers to look through each of the areas of the curriculum to see how effectively their aims were being fulfilled. A teacher might take an issue like 'the development of children's language ability' and look across various subjects and topics to see what opportunities there were for enriching reading, writing, listening and speaking. Many teachers who did this exercise found that it stimulated their awareness of what was happening in their classroom. In some cases it was revealed that 'language' was in danger of disappearing entirely as a curriculum area in its own right if they argued too strongly that it could be covered adequately in science, mathematics and humanities.

An example of a two-dimensional approach to curriculum analysis is shown below in simplified form, with three subject areas and two developmental aims running across them. When children work together to improvise a role play in their English lessons, solve a mathematical problem or conduct a science experiment, this might offer good opportunities for both language and social development.

	English	*Mathematics*	*Science*
Language			
Social skills			

Figure 7   A simple two-dimensional grid for analysing opportunities for developmental aims in three subject areas

Some writers have proposed this kind of approach for just one single subject area. Purves (1971) analysed the teaching of literature in American secondary schools. His two-dimensional scheme displayed 'Behaviour' across the top and 'Content' along the side of the grid. The 'Behaviour' categories included 'application of knowledge', 'express one's interpretation' and 'be willing to respond'. Among the 'Content' categories were examples of literary works to be studied like 'lyric poetry', 'novel' and 'belles lettres', as well as 'literary terms' and 'cultural information'. In each cell of the two-dimensional grid the teacher could record a six-point scale ranging from 'not mentioned' to 'extremely heavily emphasised'.

Several curriculum development projects have combined more than one dimension. The 1970s in particular was a decade when there were numerous large-scale curriculum development projects. Many of these incorporated a philosophy and practice which went beyond the mere listing of topics and themes. Some projects covered a combination of subjects in the curriculum, particularly in a field like humanities, when geography and history and other subjects might be combined. The ideas of Stenhouse mentioned above were put into practice in the Humanities Curriculum Project which he directed. The project made methods of teaching and learning central, rather than peripheral, as pupils discussed topics like 'the family' or 'education'. During these classroom discussions teachers were required to act as a non-directive chairman, suppressing the temptation to dominate with their own views, a role which aroused much discussion and controversy.

The Humanities Curriculum Project was an interesting illustration of a curriculum in which considerable prominence was given to process as well to content. There are several other examples, particularly in fields like science and geography. The Biological Sciences Curriculum Study (BSCS) in the United States, and the various science programmes sponsored by the Nuffield Foundation in the United Kingdom, were all notable for the emphasis they placed on guided discovery. These projects stressed that children should learn not just by being told, but by being put into a situation where they had to find out for themselves. Thus pupils might undertake an experiment, note down their results, compare what they had found with others in their class, formulate a scientific 'law', and finally check with the textbook version of that law to see whether they had 'discovered' what the scientific community knew they would discover. The argument put forward by those who designed these projects was that thinking and behaving like a real scientist was an important part of learning to be one.

Geography projects such as 'Geography 14–18' and 'Geography for the Young School-Leaver' were further examples of curriculum development projects which tried to build in methods of teaching and learning, rather than concentrate entirely on subject content and leave classroom processes to chance. However, national projects of this kind were sometimes criticised for representing a 'top down' approach to teaching, seeking to impose from above and outside a philosophy and practice that might be foreign to some teachers, leaving them alienated and lacking any sense of ownership. As a result, in a number of these process-conscious projects, teachers often adopted the subject matter, but ignored or subverted the methods.

29a Experiment
Looking for a law

Take a seesaw and balance it on the wedge at the centre. Put some loads on each side. You should put the loads at the marks so that you know when a load is one step out or two steps out or four steps out from the centre. Don't put a load $2\frac{3}{4}$ steps out because that would make it harder to find out the scientific story of seesaws. First make the seesaw balance with two piles of loads (pennies), one each side.

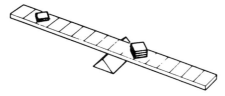

When you have it balanced, the seesaw will tip over to one side and stay there, and it will tip over to the other side and stay there. You will not be able to make it stay exactly balanced in mid-air. That is because it is sitting on top of the support at the centre, ready to fall over either way. But this will be just like 'weighing sweets': when the scales are exactly balanced and you find ever so little more would tip the scale one way or the other.

You have balanced the seesaw with two piles of pennies. *How can you move the pennies and keep the balance?*

Find out what you can about a balancing seesaw, with different loads on it. Make notes in your notebook of what happens. See if you can find out some rule or story that you could tell other people about balancing loads.

29b Experiment
Using your law

Use a large seesaw made from a plank balanced on a brick, and your knowledge of the 'lever law' to weigh your partner.

Figure 8   Children learn to look for and apply a law in physics
Source: *Nuffield Physics*, Year 1, Longman, 1978

For example, Hamilton (1975) studied the teaching of integrated science packages in which the emphasis was supposed to be on 'discovery learning'. He found that some teachers did the exact opposite of what the curriculum developers had intended.

THE CUBIC CURRICULUM

There are many dimensions to the curriculum, and in the cubic curriculum I have attempted to incorporate three of them, though there might well have been more. In order to become more familiar with this particular three-dimensional model, consider the following classroom scene, observed during a research project. In the course of this book there will be a number of 'Think Boxes'. These are nothing more than activities or incidents that can be reflected on by the reader, discussed with others, or that are subsequently dealt with in the text of this book. Here is the first of them.

 THINK BOX 1: WHICH DIMENSION OF THE CUBIC CURRICULUM?

- -

Read the description of this classroom incident and reflect on the three dimensions of the cube and how they might be manifested.

A class of twelve-year-olds is doing gymnastics in the school gymnasium. Three boys are working together, one holding a work card on which a set of movements is illustrated. Their task is to help one another improve their own performance of each movement. Two pupils are to try to work out a paired movement, as shown in the pictures they have; the third must help them do it better. They then swap roles, so that each has a chance both to perform with a partner and to coach the others.

When the third boy, Ian, takes his turn as coach to the other two pupils, he derides their performance. 'You're clueless, Gareth', Ian laughs, 'you've no idea. You're a complete Digby' ('Digby' is the name of the local mental hospital, used as a term of abuse).

The class's teacher comes over and explains patiently that the whole idea is that they should help each other improve, not just show contempt. 'See what you think is going wrong and try to come up with something constructive,' he says to Ian. 'Gareth didn't laugh at you when you were doing it.'

The two boys carry on, and Ian suggests that if Gareth straightened his back, then the movement might work better.

As a part of the school's or any individual pupil's curriculum, this event can be studied and analysed from several points of view. The first dimension of the cubic curriculum is *subject matter*. So far as this dimension is concerned, we are dealing with a lesson scheduled on the timetable as 'physical education'. Within that subject the sub-topic 'gymnastics' is a significant part of the syllabus. Inside the 'gymnastics' envelope, individual and paired movements are a legitimate element of the practical work involved.

For some people the story would end there. Yet if the word 'curriculum' is stretched to cover *all* that children learn in school, not just what appears on a timetable, then a great deal more is happening. If the first dimension of the cubic curriculum is subject matter, then the second is *cross-curricular themes*. There are some issues that spread right across the curriculum, likely to occur in any subject. Gareth and Ian are also learning something about social behaviour, specifically about 'citizenship', being a member of a wider society, in which citizens can manifest either positive or negative views and behaviour towards the performance of their fellows.

The third dimension of the cube is *teaching and learning strategies*, and in this episode we can see a number of those. Gareth, Ian and their fellow pupils are learning by imitation, since they have pictures of model gymnastics movements on their workcard and also watch one another. They are working as a team, sometimes harmoniously, sometimes not. The teacher is acting as an organiser and supporter, but intervenes in a direct way when he sees Gareth being ridiculed by Ian.

This episode shows how the model of the cubic curriculum can be used to approach analysis of classroom events from different angles. It also shows the limitation of the model. There might, for example, be further dimensions, not just the three mentioned above. These could include 'emotion' or 'mood', such as the climate of aggression,

Figure 9   Gymnastics, and social development

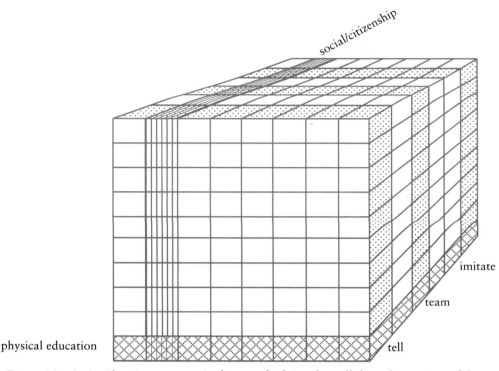

Figure 10   An incident in a gymnastics lesson which involves all three dimensions of the cubic curriculum

Key   The first dimension   'physical education'
        The second dimension 'social/citizenship'
        The third dimension   'tell', 'team' and 'imitate'

empathy, enjoyment, boredom, arousal or torpor in which pupils find themselves. Another possibility might be which of the senses was involved, whether pupils used their sight, hearing, touch, smell or taste, alone or in combination. There might be yet more dimensions which covered the many contexts in which teaching and learning can take place, or the use of educational technology and other supposed aids to learning.

The problem with having several dimensions is that, although there may be a perfectly good theoretical case for including them in a model, it is extremely difficult to visualise something with five or six dimensions. Attempts have been made to depict hyperspace on a flat, two-dimensional page, but such diagrams tend to confuse rather than clarify. A three-dimensional representation, therefore, is offered as a simplified but graspable alternative. Furthermore, there are dozens of possibilities for sub-headings along each of the dimensions in the cube. In the case of the first dimension, the subjects being studied, it would soon be possible to list 50 or 100 subjects, including traditional school subjects like 'science' and 'geography', or vocational subjects such as 'plumbing' and 'automobile repair'. *The headings in each dimension of the cubic curriculum, therefore, are illustrative rather than complete*, and possible alternatives will be discussed in more detail in the relevant chapters of this book. A cube with the measurements $50 \times 50 \times 50$ would be perfectly possible to conceive, but, with 125,000 different cells, would be a nightmare to comprehend.

There is one further, slightly dreary but inescapable technical problem with a graphic illustration such as a cube. It is possible to show, say, 10 labels clearly along the front, but not so many down the sides, which have to be foreshortened to give the 3D effect. The actual model shown in this book, therefore, is not a perfect cube, nor is it in hyperspace, as it would have to be if a fourth, fifth and sixth dimension were added. It is simply representative of something more complex and intricate beneath and within itself.

SOME TERMS AND CONCEPTS

The curriculum – what is taught and learned in schools – should be accessible to all with a legitimate interest in it: teachers, pupils, parents, governors, members of the public. I have tried to avoid, wherever possible, the sort of confusing jargon with which discussions about curriculum can be laced. There are a few terms and concepts, however, which are used, so these are explained below.

Cell

For simplicity the cubic curriculum has ten subjects, eight cross-curricular themes and six forms of teaching and learning. This makes it a $10 \times 8 \times 6$ model. In other words, there are 480 'cells', the molecules of the model. Each cell represents a combination of the dimensions. Think Box 1 above, which describes how Gareth's attempts at gymnastics are ridiculed by Ian, could be placed partly in the 'physical education – social/citizenship – imitate' cell, certainly in terms of the teacher's intention. However, when the teacher intervenes and reprimands Ian, this could equally be placed in the 'physical education – social/citizenship – tell' cell, for he is seeking to influence the boy's social development by telling him of his responsibility to be constructive when working with others.

Dimension

The term 'dimension' is used for the three major dimensions of the cube, the first dimension being the subjects, the second the cross-curricular themes, and the third dimension the forms of teaching and learning.

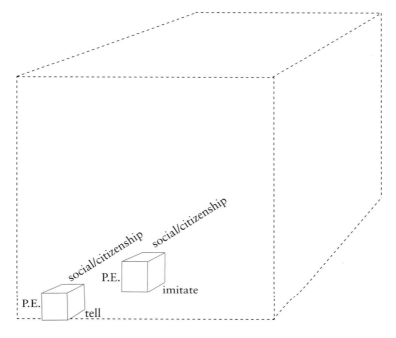

Figure 11   Two cells inside the cubic curriculum
1   The physical education – 'social/citizenship', 'tell'
2   The physical education – 'social/citizenship', 'imitate'

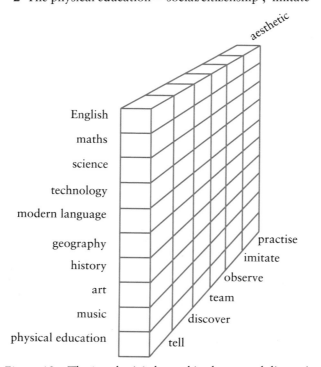

Figure 12   The 'aesthetic' channel in the second dimension

Channel

Whenever something is discussed that goes right across cells of another dimension, then the term 'channel' is used. For example, a cross-curricular theme, like the development of children's aesthetic awareness, could be found not just in art or music lessons, but when considering beautiful design (technology), attractive crystals (science), pleasing shapes (mathematics) or brilliant architecture (history). These features would thus be found along the 'aesthetic' channel.

Another example of a channel would be if a teacher decided that, in covering several subjects in the primary school curriculum, her principal strategy would be to transmit information in various fields. These transactions would then occur in the 'tell' channel of the cube, cutting right across the subjects.

Block

A 'block' of the cube covers a combination of several cells, not necessarily adjacent to each other. A simple example would be if a school decided to teach history and geography together, under the heading 'humanities'. All the cells along these two channels would then constitute the humanities 'block'. A different instance would occur in the case of several individual or pairs of cells. Suppose a primary teacher, as part of her language development policy, used a range of strategies aimed at improving children's reading ability. These might include encouraging pupils to read with one another as well as privately in a variety of forms of fiction and in non-fiction topics, reading them stories and poems, encouraging them to use the library and several other approaches. This would cover numerous cells in the cube, like the 'English – language – tell', the 'science – language – team' and the 'geography – language (and social/

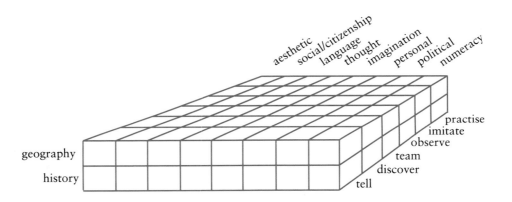

Figure 13   A 'humanities' block – integrating geography and history in the first dimension

citizenship) – discover' cells. Together these would make up the 'block' containing the teaching of reading strategies.

These terms are not meant to dominate discussion, they are nothing more than shorthand, common-sense terms for different elements of the model. This explanation is given here simply to clarify the terms used, not to confuse issues, or surround the model in mystique. The model is meant to offer a simple structure for helping teachers analyse classroom and curricular process, practice and outcome, from society's, their pupils' and their own point of view, no more and no less. If schools are to improve, then teachers and pupils will need to change what they do, first by reflecting and then by taking appropriate and intelligent action. It is hoped that the model can offer a language and structure that may facilitate reflection and action. I shall say more about the 'dynamic school' and the nature of change and improvement in education in Chapter 6.

WHICH DIMENSION?

Schools and teachers often have to make strategic decisions when constructing a curriculum. An example of this would be children's personal, social and moral development. Should this be counted as a 'subject', with its time allocation alongside maths, science and history, or should it pervade all lessons and be an integral part of them?

School A might argue that this is such an important issue that time must be assigned to it in a formal and public way. Every child would then attend lessons called 'personal, social and moral education'. A certain amount of time each week would, therefore, be allocated to the subject and this would appear in the school's formal timetable. School B, however, might believe that it is a major responsibility of *all* teachers to nurture the personal, social and moral development of their pupils. Instead of allocating time on the timetable, this school would concentrate its attention on sensitising all its teachers to ways in which they can help their pupils' growth into mature citizens.

In other words, whereas School A has chosen to place its principal effort and scrutiny along the first dimension of the cube by making the personal development a subject, School B has opted more for the second and, indeed, the third dimension of the cube, deciding to treat the matter as a cross-curricular theme requiring certain teaching styles. School C might adopt yet another strategy and combine these two approaches.

This example illustrates that *there is bound to be some degree of overlap between and within the dimensions*. It is not always possible to make a clean separation of one from another, and sometimes a particular concept or activity might be equally at home in another of the dimensions. 'Information technology', for example, can be in the first dimension as a subject given scheduled time on the timetable, during which pupils will become proficient in the use of different kinds of hardware and software. It can also be located in the second dimension as something that is likely to be used in many different subjects, so pupils will develop competence not solely in classes officially labelled 'information technology', but also in science, mathematics or English lessons. There is even a case for placing it in the third dimension, since the use of information sources other than the teacher is a legitimate teaching and learning strategy. The cubic curriculum may have clean edges in its diagrammatic 'ideal form', but in real life the lines are likely to be much more blurred.

The cubic curriculum can be rotated so that the principal focus is on events via one particular dimension, in two dimensions, or in all three. It is like looking at dice. You can hold a die in your hand and choose to look at the number three, knowing that the other five numbers are there as well, but that it is the number three that has greatest prominence. One analogy might be with contemplating a building. We can study photographs of the front, the side, or the top of the building. Seen from the front there might be a very impressive façade. Viewed from the side, however, one might notice the dustbins and the compost heap. It is still the same house, and the façade has not gone away, but the second vantage point offers a different perspective, one that may not be any more or less important, just different. An aerial picture of the house might draw attention to the state of the roof or the attractive layout of the gardens. Put the three images together and there may be enough information to construct a three-dimensional model that effectively captures the essence of the house in manageable form.

One valuable use of the cuboid model, therefore, is to focus on aspects of the curriculum along different dimensions, depending on the particular purpose in mind. Someone interested in the extent to which the officially required content is being covered might start by looking along the first dimension, to see what different individual subjects and combinations of subjects appeared to be contributing to pupils' learning, and regard the other two dimensions as a backcloth.

This raises the interesting and important issue of *control*. Some dimensions of the cubic curriculum are more amenable to influence by teachers and pupils than others. If the content of the subjects of a curriculum are tightly and precisely prescribed by some government or outside agency, then the first dimension offers less flexibility than the other two in the particular three-dimensional view put forward here. In many countries the first dimension is statutory, written down and required by law. In the case of the second dimension, cross-curricular issues are more likely to be left to schools to implement as they decide, though guidance may be given about the place of 'language' or 'thought'. The third dimension, teaching and learning strategies, is even less likely to be decided by law, though in some countries teachers of modern languages are required to teach in the foreign, rather than the native language, for example, so prescription is not impossible.

Another person studying the experiences of individual pupils might take the pragmatic view that, if there is more scope to make decisions about teaching and learning than about subject content, it would be better to begin with the third dimension, that of teaching and learning, to see what variety of practice they were exposed to over a period of time. This might reveal that pupils spent all day being passive in every branch of their studies, or that they were active, but in an unvarying way, perhaps filling in worksheets each lesson. It might show a stimulating day in which the challenges were many and the stimulus changed judiciously according to the context. It would be a mistake, however, to abandon all thoughts of looking critically at subjects simply because the matters to be taught have been decided outside the school. There is still a great deal to play for. These kinds of issues and applications will be addressed in later chapters of this book.

THE LABELS

Capturing every conceivable dimension of the cubic curriculum, each with all imaginable sub-topics, would be a near impossibility. Imagine the subject dimension alone. One could list 20, 30, 40, 100, 1000 different subjects. The same would apply to the other sides of the cube. Eventually a structure containing millions of cells would have been assembled, comprehensive perhaps, but difficult to grasp. The labels attached to each dimension of the cube in the figures in this book, therefore, are merely illustrative, for reasons given in Chapter 1.

The first dimension, the subjects of the curriculum, illustrates this point very well. It is not an actual programme of subjects such as a class or individual might follow. The cubic curriculum illustrated in this book simply takes, as exemplars, a number of the subjects often found on a school or college timetable. A purely vocational version would look completely different, and so would other curricula from other domains. Depending on the nature and degree of specialisation of the student's programme, the labels can be general subject titles, such as 'history' or 'mathematics', or in a more specialised course – say, in physical education and sport – sub-topics like 'gymnastics', 'dance', 'team games' and 'racquet sports'.

In a university degree course in 'modern languages', for example, where students are majoring in French and German, the first dimension of the cube might read: French translation, classical French tragedy, twentieth-century French novel, German translation, the plays of Goethe and Schiller, medieval German poetry, European political institutions, history of language. A vocational curriculum for an aspect of a field like 'the built environment' might need first-dimension labels such as: an introduction to electrical systems, the theory of electricity and magnetism, switches and insulators, practical circuitry and micro-electronics.

The same would apply to the other two dimensions. Cross-curricular themes could vary according to the context. For example, the undergraduate modern linguist in the example above might be developing 'critical understanding of literature' in several of the courses being studied, like the ones on classical French tragedy, the twentieth-century novel, the plays of Goethe and Schiller and medieval German poetry. Indeed, if 'critical understanding' is important, the tutors might decide to tackle it directly, by offering a taught course on 'critical theory' which would be then included in the first dimension. In the vocational course on the built environment a cross-curricular theme like 'the use of information technology' might be an important part of several courses, but it could equally be given a timetable slot as well, and thus count as a first-dimension label.

Similarly, the teaching and learning dimension might attract different labels. In the undergraduate language course it would probably be important for the students to learn to speak and listen, read and write in the foreign language. The 'in French' and 'in German' tags could, therefore, become third-dimension labels that would illuminate what kind of direct practice students were offered in the language being studied. The vocational course on the built environment might include a third-dimension feature such as 'practising specific skill', which would allow investigation of the opportunities students had to hone the sort of skills they would eventually need in their job. These issues of labelling will be taken up in more detail in the following chapters.

USING THE CUBIC CURRICULUM

There are a number of possible applications of the model, which can be used by people with different approaches to the study, design, implementation and evaluation of a curriculum. It can be a vehicle for both rational and empirical purposes. Bantock (1980) has described the significant ideological differences that can exist between the humanistic and the empirical traditions. The rational humanist approach is inspired by the beliefs of thinkers like Erasmus, who argued that the knowledge of words should precede the knowledge of things. This was an 'a priori' view of life, where instruction about human affairs, facts or empirical knowledge must come before experience of them, so that thinking and learning can be structured in advance.

This rational approach to curriculum, stressing the building in of opportunities to fulfil known or agreed objectives of teaching and learning, is in stark contrast to the empirical approach. Empiricists are influenced, indirectly perhaps, by thinkers such as Comenius, so they might concentrate on the process and outcomes of learning. Comenius said, 'men must . . . be taught to become wise by studying the heavens, the earth, oaks, and beeches, but not by studying books'. In this spirit, teachers might follow their intuitive professional sense about what they and their classes needed to do, and then reflect on what appeared to have been learned.

The cubic curriculum model can thus be used for many different purposes and by those with various viewpoints, as will be shown in Chapter 6. Someone planning a new curriculum could take the model as a stimulus to thinking widely and deeply about what might be achieved. Another person, seeking to evaluate existing practice, could look down the dimensions, individually or in combination, to appraise more broadly than is often the case what is actually happening in classrooms, as well as what sort of learning environment individual or groups of pupils experience. A third application is for a group of teachers to look at aspects of life in their classrooms as part of their own individual as well as their collective professional development. There are other possibilities.

Since the labels on the model can be changed to suit the context in which it is being applied, there are few limits to the imaginative uses to which the model can be put. Indeed, the dimensions themselves can be changed as well, and those interested in other aspects of teaching and learning than are described in this book can easily create a unique version of the model for themselves. So the cubic curriculum might be likened to a microscope when looking closely at something specific, a telescope when seeking a more distant overview, or a camera for taking and comparing snapshots from different vantage points. Since similes and metaphors can soon become pretentious and comical, or indeed collapse if taken too far, I shall not pursue these notions any further, but rather describe each of the dimensions, starting with the first one, that of the subjects on the timetable.

CHAPTER THREE

Subjects, the First Dimension

The first dimension of the cubic curriculum highlights the subjects found on a timetable. As was pointed out above, the subjects shown in the model of the cubic curriculum in this book are not meant to be a typical or ideal curriculum, as they are merely illustrative of the headings often used when a school or college timetable is assembled. Some of the subjects shown, like English, mathematics and science, are typical of what would be found in the formal curriculum of most schools in the English-speaking world. Other possible subject labels, like humanities, represent combinations of subjects, while yet others, such as construction and nursing, though they might possibly figure in a school programme, are much more likely to be seen in vocational courses, and robotics could be a subject in its own right, or a sub-topic of a larger field, like 'engineering' or 'technology'.

This chapter concentrates on looking at the curriculum principally along the subject channels, with the other two dimensions in the background. It is mainly, but not exclusively, the first dimension that usually has to cover the vast amount of human

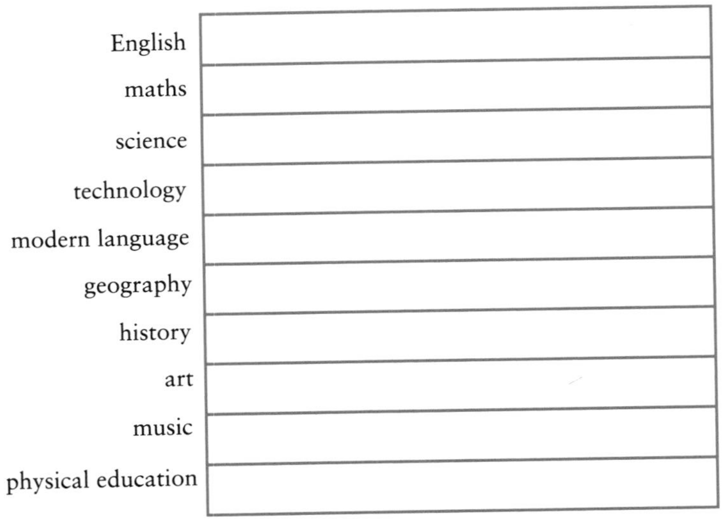

English	
maths	
science	
technology	
modern language	
geography	
history	
art	
music	
physical education	

Figure 14   The first dimension – the subjects

knowledge that teachers need to transmit to the next generation by various means. The ever-growing scope and complexity of knowledge described earlier poses difficult problems for teachers trying to prepare their classes for an uncertain future. It is not possible, in the short format of a book like this, to explore fully all the issues that might be contemplated under the heading 'subject teaching', either for traditional single subjects, or for combinations and thematic approaches, or to debate the detailed content of any one of the many subjects that might be taught. That could fill hundreds of books. It will only be feasible to raise a limited number of matters that deserve scrutiny when a curriculum is being devised or evaluated.

THE NATURE AND USES OF SUBJECT KNOWLEDGE

The subjects that are placed formally on a timetable are usually saturated with knowledge of various kinds. Life without knowledge is difficult to imagine. We should certainly not be able to cross a road in safety. It is questionable whether we could even walk properly, because, although some movements, like blinking, are automatic, walking upright over various kinds of surface is something we have learned which has then become part of our taken-for-granted knowledge. With relevant knowledge a potentially hazardous act, like crossing a road, is more often accomplished successfully than unsuccessfully. Without relevant knowledge, however, we could have no concept of danger, or of the need for vigilance, or the implications of the direction and speed of vehicles, or the quite different functions of the pavement and the road. But then, without knowledge there would be no road to cross, no pavement and no motor cars. Those who constructed them used the knowledge built up by generations of their forebears. What we know is, to a considerable extent, what we are.

Knowledge offers power and control to people, whether they wish to wield it or not. Those who understand scientific and technological fields, the law, medicine, how the political system works, can, if they wish, exercise some degree of power over those who do not, just as happened when the illiterate peasants of the past found themselves in thrall to the few in their community who could read and write. If we are told by a legal expert that what we are proposing to do is unlawful, or if we are assured by a mechanic that the state of our motor car is so fragile that only a sizeable cash payment to the garage will make it run again, then without relevant knowledge to counter what is being said, we shall probably behave as we are directed.

Knowledge is freedom. Possession of it does not guarantee complete freedom, of course, but it does offer us more control over our own affairs than we would otherwise have. Knowledge gives us the freedom to make choices on the basis of accurate information; to travel to places that we know of, or where someone is willing to offer us a salary in return for our skills; to direct our own lives, rather than have to wait around for others to act on our behalf; to find out even more than we know already, building on existing knowledge, extending autonomy.

Education is a continuous and timeless human process, stretching from the past through the present and into the future. It is the vehicle by means of which the wisdom and experiences accumulated over several millennia are transported to the next and following generations. By the end of their period of compulsory schooling most children will have acquired pieces of knowledge that took countless lifetimes to compile. The information that water consists of two atoms of hydrogen and one atom of oxygen can be transmitted by a teacher in seconds, yet several thousand years of human existence preceded its discovery. The painstaking researches of hundreds of historians, archivists and archaeologists can be synthesised and interpreted to numerous others by one skilful communicator. Teachers can accelerate human intellectual development, distil the essence of immense periods of exploration and discovery into a few years, enabling young people to build on and extend what their predecessors knew.

Knowledge comes in many different forms. Much of it has been coded and compiled under well-established headings, like 'science', 'history' or 'mathematics'. Some of it is part of the intimate and often seamless relationship between knowledge and skills, forming the vital foundation on which people draw in order to practise human skills: the knowledge of electricity that informs the practice of the competent electrician, the understanding of the workings of the human body needed by a surgeon, the accumulated wisdom about human behaviour that influences how we relate to one another in our various social groups. When the relevant knowledge is missing, it is

Figure 15   Education allows children to acquire knowledge that took countless lifetimes to
compile
(*Photo courtesy of Exeter College*)

often embarrassingly evident how important it is: the poor linguist who cannot communicate with others, the innumerate cashier who gives customers too much or too little change, the amateur electrician who wires a plug incorrectly, perhaps with fatal results.

In Chapter 1 the implications were discussed of the massive explosion of knowledge which continues to gather pace unremittingly. Children will need a wide range of knowledge so that they can function effectively in the complex future that they face. They will require basic competence in several areas, not just literacy and numeracy; higher competence in different fields; the ability and willingness to find out for themselves if they are to be autonomous, as well as to make expertise available to others. In terms of subject knowledge, they will also need both highly specialised, detailed knowledge of certain specific fields, as well as a general grasp of the basic foundation concepts in those same and other areas. It is not easy to map out the full programme of what may be necessary.

In the circumstances, it is sometimes asserted that in the twenty-first-century knowledge will no longer have the importance it once held. The two reasons for this that are commonly given are first that a great deal of knowledge soon becomes out of date in a rapidly changing society, and second that knowledge can in any case be stored on immense databases, so there is no reason for it to be committed to memory, since it can easily be retrieved from increasingly lightweight and portable machines.

That knowledge will have little importance is a dangerous misconception. Just because the discovery of information is escalating apace does not mean that it must not be chased. There are hundreds of thousands of words in the English language, and the total increases every day as new words are coined and added, while relatively few slide away. This is not regarded as an argument against having a comprehensive and growing vocabulary. Doctors are faced with huge amounts of fresh knowledge about the human body and they too have access to vast reservoirs of electronically stored information. Nobody seriously puts forward the case that they will need little working day-to-day knowledge in the twenty-first century. Indeed, there is a strong case for arguing that the more knowledge there is, the *more* people need to embrace as much of it as they can.

This need for constant and rapid updating also highlights the importance of certain kinds of knowledge. For example, the *organising concepts and skills* of a subject, those fundamental ideas and techniques that form the core of it, become the important bedrock on which discrete pieces of fresh information or new technique can be grounded. If there is a new theory of the structure of the atom which outdates previous theories, then it will be lost on those who have no concept of what an atom actually is. Should someone develop a new way of swimming faster, then it will be learned most easily by those who are proficient swimmers, rather than by people who cannot swim at all. Giving priority to the acquisition of these central precepts may be an important prerequisite of being able to cope with the future. In addition, since even what are regarded at any particular time as 'key concepts' may one day become expendable and ephemeral, pupils may need to have the flexibility and elasticity of mind to discard them, however difficult they were to acquire in the first place.

In terms of perceived needs, much of the discussion about subject knowledge is bound to be as vague as is speculation about an uncertain future. Take, for example, a subject like mathematics. The mathematics that most people use in adult life is in a very restricted field, mainly to do with number. Whether there will be significantly higher mathematical demands on citizens in the future is not easy to predict. For some who use mathematics in their work, greater competence may well be required, as has happened in a field like engineering. In other cases the widespread availability of calculators might, on the surface, appear to have reduced the need for arithmetical competence. Yet people unable to work out sums manually may make elementary place errors. For example, the simple sum $816 \div 4$ is often answered with an erroneous '24', rather than the correct '204' by those unable to grasp the concept of place value. Someone innumerate who makes an error keying figures into a calculator will accept uncritically whatever emerges as the answer. Automation does not remove the need for understanding, it may even enhance it.

At present, however, the daily experience of the majority ventures little way beyond the elementary mental arithmetic or estimation involved in addition, subtraction, multiplication and division. Common operations related to a shopping trip include the addition of the cost of items purchased, the subtraction of money from one's capital when payments are made, the division of articles or commodities when these are shared out, and the use of multiplication when several identically priced items are purchased at the same time. Some of these simple, everyday transactions are often based on quick rough and ready estimates, rather than exact calculation. Shapes and elementary statistics may make an occasional impact, if people are choosing floor tiles, or studying crime figures, but adult life is not littered with quadratic equations, Euclidian theorems and the calculation of correlations. Even in terms of what is learned in primary school, few people ever do a long division sum by hand once they have left school. A mathematics, history or science course based solely on what are thought to be the demands of adult life, therefore, would tend to be narrow, brief and functional.

One argument often put forward for a perspective on the curriculum that is wider than equipping children solely with what they are thought to need, is that education should train the mind. This view is based on two assumptions: (1) that what pupils learn is transferable, so their learning can in future be applied in a range of situations and circumstances, and (2) that the mind is an infinitely elastic vessel that benefits from being stretched, rather than left limp.

The evidence for both transfer and elasticity is not always conclusive, but there are numerous examples where what is learned in one situation can be helpful in another, particularly if the key concepts involved are fully understood. Those who have learned one musical instrument and then wish to learn to play a second one will usually be able to transfer such skills as the ability to read music. The obverse of 'transfer', however, is 'interference'. Someone who knows Spanish might well find another Romance language, like Italian, easier to learn, but there will also be interference, causing some learners to confuse the Italian definite article *il* with the Spanish one *el*.

The evidence for the 'elasticity' of mind is particularly marked in older people.

Elderly stroke victims can still learn substantially different skills with appropriate teaching, which help them compensate for the loss of competence caused by their illness. Mental activity generally in old age is thought to be positively associated with physical and emotional good health. The positive feature of the human race is that most members of it, though they may believe to the contrary, are only too old to learn when the coffin lid is finally screwed down on them.

KNOWLEDGE PLUS

Useful though knowledge may be, on its own it can often have limited value. Knowledge of facts without understanding of their significance, value, relationships, application, frailty or certainty, is of limited value, like bricks without cement. When studying a particular subject or interdisciplinary topic, children usually need much more than knowledge alone, and they often have to learn skills, attitudes and values, and forms of behaviour. In the case of a topic like dental care in a programme of health education, for example, children might indeed learn pieces of knowledge (why teeth can cause pain, how to avoid tooth decay), but they may well learn skills (how to brush their teeth properly), attitudes and values (the desire to avoid dental decay, the importance of regular dental checks), and pieces of behaviour (establishing healthy routines, like cleaning the teeth after meals and making regular visits to the dentist). Mere possession of knowledge about the effects of plaque will do nothing to avoid toothache, nor will having the skill of cleaning teeth properly unless it is applied. In the end the real test of a health programme is not just what people know, but what they do. A successful outcome is the result of a combination of factors, which may well start with knowledge, but must also embrace skills, attitudes and values, and actual behaviour.

This wider view of the first dimension of the cubic curriculum opens up a considerable discussion. One important issue is the extent to which, if children are learning skills as well as knowledge, their curriculum should be angled towards the job or jobs they might eventually take in adult life. The debate about an applied or vocational, versus a liberal humanist curriculum, has been rehearsed many times. The English tradition in the twentieth century was for most schools' curricula to be principally 'liberal' in nature, so subjects like 'journalism' or 'driver education', which might be found in an American high school, have usually been absent.

In the early 1980s, however, the English tradition changed with the introduction of the Technical and Vocational Education Initiative in 1983. Most secondary schools began to teach a programme of pre-vocational education. Uncertainty about the future of employment meant that these courses did not usually attempt to prepare pupils for a single named job – that would have been too risky in the unpredictable labour market which had seen thousands of apprenticeships disappear. In Germany, by contrast, though unemployment worsened during the 1980s, apprenticeships and high-quality vocational education in institutions like the *Berufschule* survived. The emphasis in Britain, however, was more on the broad skills thought to be useful for

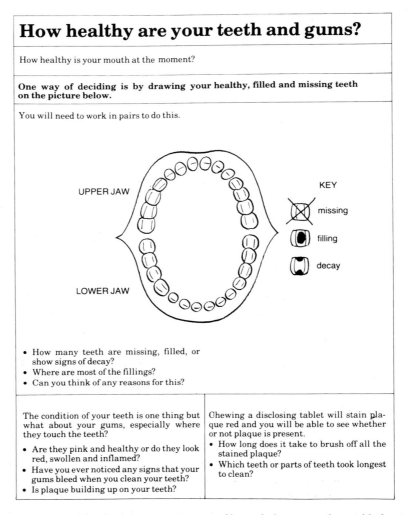

How healthy are your teeth and gums?

How healthy is your mouth at the moment?

One way of deciding is by drawing your healthy, filled and missing teeth on the picture below.

You will need to work in pairs to do this.

UPPER JAW

KEY

missing

filling

decay

LOWER JAW

- How many teeth are missing, filled, or show signs of decay?
- Where are most of the fillings?
- Can you think of any reasons for this?

The condition of your teeth is one thing but what about your gums, especially where they touch the teeth?

- Are they pink and healthy or do they look red, swollen and inflamed?
- Have you ever noticed any signs that your gums bleed when you clean your teeth?
- Is plaque building up on your teeth?

Chewing a disclosing tablet will stain plaque red and you will be able to see whether or not plaque is present.

- How long does it take to brush off all the stained plaque?
- Which teeth or parts of teeth took longest to clean?

Figure 16   Health education – a mixture of knowledge, attitudes and behaviour
Source: *Smile, please!* Forbes Publications, 1982

a cluster of jobs in the 'caring professions' or the 'built environment'. Surveys of the opinions of employers have often suggested that they prefer new recruits to have received a good general education during which not only basic knowledge has been acquired, but also personal characteristics, like flexibility, willingness to learn, reliability and punctuality have been encouraged. Dunne and Bennett (1996) cite examples from graduate recruitment literature that emphasise such personal qualities, like this one from British Gas:

We'll be looking for people who can be described as 'flexible',... You'll actively seek out new experiences.... You'll be open-minded and not afraid to challenge the way things are done. Independence is important because in this fast-changing organisation, you may not always have clear paths and procedures to follow.

Another issue to be faced in the first dimension of the cubic curriculum is the matter of breadth and depth, and the related notion of 'balance'. The expression 'broad and balanced' is more likely to be used in official curriculum documentation than its polar opposite, 'narrow and unbalanced'. There is a belief that children must explore some of the breadth of what is known, rather than be confined to just one or two subjects, hence the argument about the narrowness of the English school curriculum for 16- to 19-year-olds, with its concentration on three subjects, compared with the broader diet offered to students in most other European countries.

Breadth and depth are not mutually exclusive concepts, however. It is perfectly possible for pupils to study several subjects, some of which are pursued in greater depth. Indeed, any single subject may be broadly or narrowly conceived. Science in the primary school in some countries consists largely of nature study, possibly with a few physics concepts, but little or no chemistry. Another country's primary science curriculum may include biology, chemistry, physics, astronomy, geology, climatology and scientific method.

USING THE CUBE IN THE FIRST DIMENSION

If a country has a National Curriculum, then it may seem pointless to look at the subjects being taught. It could easily be said that if the government, or some central curriculum agency, has laid down the form a school curriculum should take, then there is nothing left to debate, as the key decisions about content have been made elsewhere. Yet there is far more to the subject dimension than the syllabus alone. Some teachers may be more influenced in the manner they teach the curriculum by the layout and emphasis of the textbook they use, than by the original curriculum document, especially if they work their way through the book in page sequence. Detailed day-to-day decisions about a curriculum are often still there for teachers to take, even when their syllabus is externally determined. In this and the next two chapters I propose to look at ways in which the curriculum can be considered starting from one particular dimension of the cube as the principal vantage point, with the other dimensions more in the background. In the final chapter of the book I shall discuss ways in which all the dimensions can be combined.

There are many ways of studying or changing the curriculum by taking the first dimension of the cube as a starting point. In those countries where there is no National Curriculum it is possible to start with a clean sheet, and map in the subjects and topics that are thought to be important. In other countries this may already have been done, but the whole of the week may not be occupied by the National Curriculum, and there may be 'free' time, at the disposal of the school, in which independent decisions can still be made. In many places, including those Eastern European countries where there has been strong state control over content, methodology, ideology and textbooks, there have been attempts to create more school autonomy, so that greater decision making and commitment can be generated at individual school and classroom level. Even with a prescriptive National Curriculum there is often some latitude for imagination and choice, particularly about where to place emphasis and what topics to amplify.

Content and key concepts

Within any single subject there is considerable debate about what elements of it should be taught at what ages. Should history emphasise people or events? When teaching about the American Civil War, should the emphasis be placed more on the Presidents, Jefferson Davis and Abraham Lincoln, and Generals Lee and Grant, or on the political issues, the events, the aftermath? When studying the arrival of the Normans in England, should pupils pay most attention to King William and King Harold, their personalities, aspirations, achievements, mistakes, or to the actual Battle of Hastings and the tactics used, the purposes behind and the procedures used to assemble the Domesday Book, the impact of French language and customs? In studying science, should younger pupils concentrate on topics closest to their interest and experience, like plants and animals, electricity and its applications, the uses and properties of materials like plastics, or should they study concepts that might be a bit more theoretical, such as the structure of the atom? These dilemmas are usually resolved not by choosing one or other extreme option, but by making judgements about different kinds of emphasis.

This raises the matter of what are the actual key *organising concepts and skills* in a particular subject. The point was made above that, in our rapidly moving society, these may be crucial pegs on which pupils can hang new subject knowledge when they encounter it. Teachers become the 'annotators' here, seeking out and identifying with their students the essential concepts that need to be learned, and then checking whether they have in fact been learned and understood, and can be applied and modified.

When teaching a topic like 'insects', there are four essential features of the central concept that need to be considered.

- The *language* and labels that are needed, like 'antennae', or 'feelers' in simpler form.
- The *attributes* of insects, the characteristics that put them into that particular class of creatures, and these can be divided into '*must have*' (essential features like 'six legs', 'three parts to the body') and '*may have*' (features which occur in some instances, but are not essential, such as 'dark colouring', or 'hard body shell').
- *Examples* of the members or occurrences of the concept (like 'flies', 'beetles') can help understanding.
- *Rules* that govern the concept (insects have six legs, a head, thorax and abdomen, two antennae and two or four wings), including whether the rules are flexible or invariable.

A concept like 'insects' is in the scientific domain and may be clearly definable, therefore, compared with the sometimes more diffuse, less easily agreed concepts that may be encountered in other subject areas, like 'fairness' or 'quality'. None the less, mapping out, exploring and acquiring key organising concepts and skills is a prime responsibility of teachers and pupils in any curriculum preparing people for the future.

Posner (1995) put forward five different perspectives on the content of the curriculum:

Traditional The principal purpose ascribed to the subjects on the curriculum is to transmit the cultural heritage of the nation and the world, so there is emphasis on what seem to be timeless facts, concepts, laws, skills. The basic skills of reading, writing and computation will be stressed, as will the vocabulary and terminology of each subject, the key dates and facts, and the predominant methodology used in the discipline. There will also be a prominent place for values, such as honesty and respect for authority, which are thought to be essential for the smooth running of society.

Experiential Strongly influenced by the writings of John Dewey (1938), the experiential curriculum starts with the subject matter closest to children's direct experience. This can then be used as a springboard for learning about what Dewey described as 'those things within the range of existing experience that have the promise

Figure 17   Learning the essential features of the concept 'insects'
Source: *Explaining*, Wragg and Brown, Routledge, 1993

and potentiality of presenting new problems which by stimulating new ways of observation and judgment will expand the area of further experience'. Thus history is studied to allow children to understand the present and speculate about the future. Science is used to explore the scientific principles that lie behind everyday applications, including the effects and outcomes of these, such as raising living standards or polluting the environment.

Structure of the disciplines This approach places emphasis on each individual subject and its structure, assumptions, theories, methods of enquiry. Pupils, therefore, become mini-experts in each subject and are eventually able to conduct their own enquiries in the field using the knowledge and tools they have acquired. When the total curriculum is put together, the cumulative effect of becoming proficient in several major subjects should ensure proper development of the mind, it is argued.

Behavioural The behavioural perspective gives highest prominence to the setting of objectives and the testing of measurable outcomes. The content of each subject is seen primarily in terms of identifiable and discrete pieces of behaviour, sometimes labelled 'competencies' or 'processes'. This view has been particularly popular in vocational education, where the separate skills and sub-skills thought to be needed in a particular job are listed and ticked when thought to have been achieved. It is a philosophy that has also been used in traditional school subjects, like mathematics. Exponents spell out in advance what operations children should be able to perform at the end of the course or unit, such as the ability to multiply two two-digit numbers, or convert a fraction to a decimal.

Cognitive Here the emphasis is on the development of children's minds by making them think and reason within each subject. Problem solving is stressed, as is writing about a subject to clarify one's understanding of its major concepts. An example of a cognitively oriented curriculum is the Reading Recovery programme developed by Marie Clay (1985), in which children's own reading strategies are developed. They are each given an individual programme in which they are encouraged to build on what is already meaningful to them. The teacher monitors the development of each child's strategies and then increases the level of difficulty as progress is made, until the pupil is able to return to the regular class.

This last example, the Reading Recovery programme, shows how focusing on the first dimension of the cubic curriculum can highlight the subject matter most prominently (learning to read in English), but keep firmly in view the second dimension of the cubic curriculum (the development of children's language and thinking) as well as the third dimension (teaching children to use their own strategies when reading new books).

Level and sequence

Some subjects, like mathematics and modern languages, are sometimes said to be more *linear* in nature than others. Unless you know A, it is argued, you cannot learn B. If you do not understand a sum like $9 \div 3$, then you are unlikely to cope with $x \div y$ when

THINK BOX 2: WHAT DOES THE CURRICULUM CONTAIN?

- -

There are many ways in which the content of the curriculum can be analysed and many purposes for doing such an exercise. Here are just some possibilities:

1 **Perspectives** Take Posner's five perspectives described above – *traditional, experiential, structure of the disciplines, behavioural, cognitive* – and see to what extent the curriculum of the class or school you are concerned with reflects any or all of these categories. Is there a need to alter or take different perspectives in any way? If so, for what reason, and what would need to be done?

2 **Content** Look at the *balance* and *breadth/depth* of the curriculum on offer. Is the curriculum too skewed? Too narrow? Too broad and lacking in depth? Or does it reflect the sort of scope that seems reasonable for the context in which it operates? Do all students have full access to it, or do some miss out? If so, why?

3 **Overlap and omission** Is there unnecessary duplication? Are there important omissions? For example, are 'geology' or 'climatology' taught in both 'science' and 'geography' lessons, or in neither? If in both, do the lessons complement or contradict each other? What steps need to be taken to rectify any problems encountered?

you move on to algebra. Similarly, those unable to say 'the man' (*der Mann*) in German will not be able to move on to the use of adjectives and say 'the old man' (*der alte Mann*). The same argument can actually be applied to any subject. If you do not know what happened in the First World War, it could be said, you will not fully understand the outbreak of the Second World War. If you do not understand the nature of hydrogen and oxygen atoms, then you will not grasp the structure of molecules of water. It was this kind of thinking that led to the notion of 'mastery learning', the view that key concepts in each subject area could be identified, learned, tested and then built on.

When looking at subject teaching in the curriculum, the issues of *level* and *sequence* are important concepts. Without any notion of what constitutes appropriate levels of work for different classes or individuals, the curriculum would be a rambling meander through random topics that were unrelated to the pupil's previous learning. There would be no difference between what is learned by 6-year-olds and 16-year-olds.

There are problems associated with trying to determine what level of work might be undertaken. The first is the matter of 'readiness'. There is a view, put forward in the Plowden Report (1967) on primary education, for example, that one should not attempt to teach children anything until they are 'ready' for it. The Report stated: 'Until a child is ready to take a particular step forward, it is a waste of time to try to teach him to take it.' This assumption was based on a too deferential view of Jean Piaget's stage theory (Piaget 1954), which stated that children progressed through various stages of intellectual development in a fixed sequence.

The counter-argument to all this is that, if you had to wait until people are thought to be fully ready before teaching anything, then (1) you might not know when this moment eventually came, (2) you could easily miss it, (3) it might be difficult to teach anybody anything for fear of attempting it too early, so expectations could become too low, (4) you would fail to capitalise on children's intuitive understanding. This last point is most important. Children can often have a quite powerful intuitive grasp of concepts which are thought to be beyond them.

Children's intuitive thinking is still inadequately understood. It may well be that many are capable of thought and action that is way in advance of what is commonly regarded as being possible for their age group. A good example of this was the phenomenon of the Rubik Cube, a six-sided cube with 25 coloured squares on each surface. The task was to twist the cube around until each side showed 25 squares of the same colour. Adults were frequently mystified, while many young children could twist and turn the cube, often using complex-looking strategies they were unable to describe, and resolve the puzzle in a very short time, perhaps as little as two minutes.

Hughes (1983) showed that pre-school children could invent their own ways of coping with numerical transactions even before they had learned formal mathematical symbols and transactions. Capitalising on early intuitive understanding can give pupils initial familiarity with something they can then tackle in greater depth at a later date, though there is a caveat, which is mentioned below.

Closely related to the idea of level are two other concepts often mentioned when the quality of teaching is being evaluated: namely, *matching* and *differentiation*. Matching is the attempt that teachers should make to match the work they set to the ability and state of knowledge, usually of the individual pupil, though it might be of a group. This may involve setting different levels or types of work for different pupils or small groups within the class, a process known as 'differentiation'. It is well worth investigating whether differentiation actually takes place or is merely rhetoric. One way of studying this is described by Neville Bennett and his colleagues (1984), whose seminal research into the quality of pupils' learning experience showed a frequent mismatch between the tasks children were given and what they seemed to be capable of when interviewed. The researchers analysed the tasks undertaken in class by 6- and 7-year-olds, and they concluded:

> In both number and language work at infant level teachers were able to provide a match on appropriately 40% of tasks. About a third were too difficult for the child and a little over a quarter were too easy.

Figure 18   Matching the maths task to the pupil

The related issue of *sequence* is also worthy of scrutiny. This is to do with the flow of learning from one level to the next, based on a judgement about the extent to which there is a logic to the order in which topics are to be studied. To give a simple example, one teacher might teach about the Romans, the Saxons, the Vikings and the Normans in chronological sequence, arguing that, until you have understood the Romans, you cannot comprehend what the Saxons brought to Britain, and so on. Another teacher might see the logical sequence as being *backwards*. Such a teacher would start with the Normans, and then move backwards in time showing how the other invaders and settlers preceded them. Taken to an extreme, however, such a view would mean that a subject like history could only be taught either by commencing with the present day and sweeping back to the origins of humanity and beyond, or vice versa.

In practice the day-to-day matter of sequencing is often more of a small-scale issue for teachers, involving decisions about two or three topics rather than the whole of the discipline. It does, however, raise a related point, which is the notion of *revisiting* topics taught. The problem with many subject curricula is that there is an assumption that every topic need only be studied on a single occasion. Once this has been done then the topic is 'in the bag', captured in the pupil's mind for ever.

Would that this were so! Although I have advocated that teachers should capitalise on children's early intuitive understanding, there is a caveat to bear in mind. Concepts learned early in life may be ill-digested. Intuitive understanding may lead to misconceptions, as well as to early insights. Hence the argument often advanced that many adults have an 8-year-old's view of the Romans or the Anglo-Saxons, and so are not familiar with the full significance of their literature, arts or institutions, such as the Witanagemot, the council of kings that was a forerunner of the English Parliament. Bruner (1960) described this need to revisit topics later in schooling, in order to gain a more mature understanding of them, as 'the spiral curriculum', which permits pupils to circle round topics, but in an upwards direction.

 THINK BOX 3: LEVEL AND SEQUENCE

- -

In the demanding world of the twenty-first century today's children will need higher levels of achievement than their forebears. Yet one of the most common criticisms of teaching is that teachers' and pupils' own expectations often seem to be too low. There are numerous ways of addressing this issue, either for a whole school or class, or for individual pupils. Possibilities include:

1 **Is the level right?**   Choose three or more children of different abilities. Look at a task in which they are engaged and talk to them about it, seeing if they can cope with a more difficult step up, or need the task simplifying. Bennett and his colleagues (1984), whose work is described above, found that more able children were often set less exacting work than they could have coped with, while pupils of lower ability were frequently given tasks that were beyond them. It is easy to behave like a sheepdog, trying to keep all pupils at or near the middle point of the ability range in the class. To what extent is the teacher able to differentiate and set tasks appropriate to the pupil concerned?

2 **Sequence**   Choose one particular subject or thematic area in the curriculum. Look at the order in which topics within it are being studied. Do they seem to be in a logical sequence? If not, how can the programme of work be changed to create more coherence?

Teachers' subject knowledge

If teachers' own knowledge of subject matter is insecure, then they will have difficulties teaching it to others. This can be a problem at all stages of education, particularly when teachers are working away from their major specialism, but it is readily apparent in primary education, when a teacher with a strong background in certain fields may be required on a regular basis to teach other subjects in which the foundations are less secure. The Leverhulme Primary Project (Wragg, 1993) identified teachers who were teaching the science topic 'electricity' to primary-age pupils without themselves having a firm grasp of the concepts involved. Some of the teachers observed in the project confessed their ignorance to the class immediately. One began, 'Look, I've got to be honest with you. I know nothing about electricity. I can just about change a fuse.'

When children could not make the bulb in their circuit light up, she had to refer them to their printed instructions, as she was not able to help. Some groups needed three or four attempts before their circuit worked properly. In interview afterwards she felt the main advantage of her ignorance had been to throw children on their own resources. An expert might have pointed out to the group experiencing difficulty that they had put some batteries into the circuit the wrong way round, and that the wires had been wrongly attached to the bulb. This would have solved the children's problem for them, whereas her own lack of subject knowledge had made them think for themselves and reach their own solution. The major disadvantage, however, is that teachers lose credibility if they have to confess their own ignorance too frequently, and in some fields the teacher's lack of knowledge could be critical – 'Today we are going to study brain surgery. I know nothing about brain surgery, but here's a scalpel, there's a brain. . . .'

What was interesting about the Leverhulme Project was the steps that teachers took to plug gaps in their own subject knowledge. Most of the problems tend not to occur before lessons, when teachers can use reference books to check their facts, or assemble resources, like books and kits, for pupils to work with, but rather during lessons, when children may encounter unanticipated difficulties, or ask unexpected questions.

I am not a science specialist, and the first time I ever taught science to primary-age children I began by asking the class of 7-year-olds if there were any questions they would like to ask me, having explained that science was about 'the world around us'. Within 30 seconds I was asked, 'Why are cars made of metal?', 'Why does smoke come out of the back of a motor bike?', 'Why does it snow?' and 'Why does a wagtail wag its tail?' All I needed was a couple of lifetimes back at the university with the professors of science and engineering, for I was as competent to answer some of the queries as I was to perform a sub-frontal leucotomy. So that was enough of the pupil-centred approach! Instead we did a topic on 'energy', since that was the one I had carefully prepared the night before.

Teaching and learning strategies will be dealt with more fully in Chapter 5, when the third dimension of the cubic curriculum is discussed, but there are strategic issues attached to the whole issue of teaching subject matter from what may be an inadequate base, or from the unpredictable questions that pupils may ask. Evading the issue and shifting onto what for the teacher is safer ground are two of a number of strategies teachers use to cope with inadequate subject knowledge.

The answers to pupils' questions may well be found in reference books, but inside the classroom most teachers were perplexed by not knowing the relevant scientific principles, and so being unable to look up the answers in a book. 'When you put sand in water, why does most of it sink, but one or two grains float?' one pupil asked his teacher. The answer is because of 'surface tension', a tensioning force which occurs on the surface of a liquid, causing the molecules to cling to one another. The effect is like having a very thin skin on the surface which holds small objects, so isolated grains of sand may float while clusters will sink. 'Floating and sinking' is not an easy topic for someone who is not a science specialist, and pupils will readily ask questions which require the teacher to have an understanding of such concepts as 'surface tension' or 'Archimedes' principle'. In the Leverhulme Project it was found that primary teachers most preferred to consult other people, such as a specialist subject co-ordinator, governors, parents even, who possessed the knowledge they lacked and so could give them a tailored answer to a specific question.

Although the problem of inadequate subject knowledge is at its most marked among primary teachers who have to cover a wide range of subjects single-handedly, it can be a difficulty at all age levels. Nor is the problem confined to subjects like science, or to primary teachers alone. There are teachers in secondary, further and higher education whose own knowledge has become out of date, or who find themselves having to teach topics away from their major specialism.

Given the explosion in knowledge that was described in earlier chapters of this book it is hardly surprising that even the most proficient and knowledgeable teachers will sometimes be caught out by inquisitive students. Indeed, part of the difficulty of living in a world where knowledge accretes at a phenomenal rate is that it can be difficult even to know precisely what one does not know. Being able and willing to keep abreast of new subject matter, to search for replies to probing questions, as well as to steer students to find their own relevant information to answer their queries themselves are important teacher attributes in these circumstances.

THINK BOX 4: TEACHERS' SUBJECT KNOWLEDGE

Rather than flagellate oneself or others for inadequate subject knowledge, it is probably wiser to regard the problem as endemic in our knowledge-laden society and consider ways of coping with the problem. Among several possibilities are the following:

1 **Personal knowledge** What aspects of a subject, or of different subjects, are you weakest in? How can the gaps be filled?

2 **Strategies** What do you do when a pupil asks a question you cannot answer? Evade it? Move the discussion onto home territory where you feel more secure? Become threatened and bridle at the questioner, or at the class? Promise to come back with the answer? Show questioners how to obtain answers for themselves? Are you content with these strategies, or should they be altered?

3 **Sources and resources** What sources of help are available? Books? People? Interactive databases? If you know of these, how can you use them most effectively? If there appear to be no such people and material resources, can any be found? One school recruited a team of local people, including parents and governors, who were willing to answer questions on the phone. Teachers in a primary school noted down questions they were unable to answer and then had a meeting once a month with a science teacher in a local secondary school to discuss and explore some of them. They also phoned up when an urgent answer was needed.

CHAPTER FOUR

Cross-curricular Issues, the Second Dimension

The second dimension of the cubic curriculum highlights the issues and domains that go right across the subject curriculum. As in the previous chapter, *the labels attached to each of the dimensions of the cubic curriculum shown in this book are illustrative, not exclusive.* Some of the headings shown, like aesthetic education, might be more prominent in some schools or in certain subjects, while others, such as social education, could be found in the first dimension if they appeared as a subject on a school's timetable, perhaps under the label 'citizenship'. Once again it is not possible to treat all such themes exhaustively in a book of this kind, so a few illustrative examples, like language and thought, will be discussed to show how they make an impact on the whole curriculum, and also how such matters might be addressed.

This chapter concentrates on looking at the curriculum mainly along the channels that reflect issues, concerns and the development of personal and social qualities that can apply to several contexts, with the other two dimensions in the background. It is the second dimension that often covers the vast amount of human competence and understanding that traverse and sometimes transcend the publicly labelled topics being studied. It can include what is sometimes called the 'hidden curriculum' as well as the official one. As was discussed in the previous chapters, the increasing

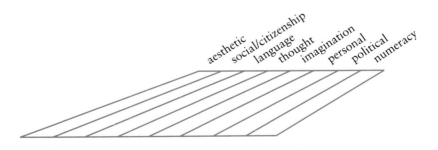

Figure 19 The second dimension – cross curricular issues

complexity of human society in the present and the future requires the development not just of children's knowledge and understanding, but also of personal qualities and characteristics, like determination, flexibility, imagination and sociability. Vital foundations for a very long lifetime in the next millennium are being laid down during the first phases of education, so it is important to study their acquisition.

The great difficulty with these cross-subject channels is that they become the awesome responsibility of every teacher. Although many teachers enjoy the fuller professional role of developing children's personality or social behaviour, others take on a wider assignment less gladly, and it is quite common for teachers to complain in particular about having to cope with especially unruly pupils, sometimes with severe personal problems. The statement 'I am a teacher, not a social worker' has been made at more than one teacher union conference. Yet few teachers would say that, just because they are, for example, a specialist teacher of science, they will take no responsibility for training their students to think when they are in a science laboratory, for where else is scientific thinking to be learned? There may be arguments about the extent to which teachers should be responsible for children's general development, but few teachers would refuse to explain a technical term in their subject, or deal with misbehaviour when it occurred, on the grounds that language and social development were entirely someone else's responsibility.

Another difficulty is the problem of gaining an overview across the many subjects and themes, projects and activities found in a typical school, both within the classroom and outside it. In a secondary school, for example, it is much easier to look at one teacher's work in mathematics, history or German, than to contemplate the extent to which 10 different teachers of 14-year-olds, as well as hundreds of other pupils, may influence students' language and thought, in the classroom, workshop, gymnasium and playground. Even in a primary school, where the same teacher may teach all the subject work, it is more straightforward to observe what is done by the teacher under the heading 'art' or 'English', than it is to analyse the across-the-board contribution to children's aesthetic or language development made formally and informally by teachers, the head, classroom assistants, parent helpers or fellow pupils.

Despite the difficulties faced when trying to evaluate a pupil's education from different perspectives, it is still worth while trying to gain the fuller picture. If personal attributes and social competence are important, then we must try and see how well pupils are being prepared for the complex world in which these qualities will be essential rather than optional. The argument is not whether the cross-curricular dimension is more or less important than the other two dimensions of the curriculum discussed here, but what it consists of, and how effective a contribution it makes to children's development.

LOOKING ACROSS THE CURRICULUM

A distinction needs to be made between different types of cross-curricular elements. In this chapter I do not want to concentrate too much on the quite legitimate matter of interdisciplinary subjects – that is, topic areas and themes, such as 'humanities', 'environmental education', 'media studies' or 'integrated science' – that simply combine and permute familiar academic and vocational subjects. Radnor (1994), among others, has written a thorough account of these. The reason for not giving this a high priority is because such subject combinations belong more in the first dimension of the cubic curriculum, as they are usually 'public', in the sense that they are there to be seen on the timetable, effectively a 'subject', albeit in conglomerate form.

In exploring the second dimension I propose to concentrate more on those overarching concepts, like the development of language, thinking or aesthetic sensibility, which can indeed be scheduled as subjects on the timetable, but are assumed to be present in a number of disciplines. Such elements are often thought to be related to the education of the 'whole person', as they nurture human competence, as well as help fashion attributes and traits, which not only influence behaviour, but also lay foundations for future learning. Inability to read, write, communicate orally, reason logically, imagine, understand people and ideas would seriously inhibit children's opportunities throughout their lives and reduce their capacity to learn what is necessary in all aspects of the curriculum, not just in particular subjects like English or mathematics.

These overarching notions raise significant questions about the first dimension of the cubic curriculum, especially about the place of each of them in the formal and informal structure of the curriculum. Where should children's aesthetic development take place? Only in the classroom? Surely not, otherwise children would never take part in or see a play, attend or participate in a concert, watch or make a film, or visit an art exhibition. Should aesthetic awareness be encouraged solely in lessons called 'art' or 'music'? In that case, what about science and mathematics? Is there nothing of beauty in these? Of course there is, and in practice the curriculum is full of opportunities to appreciate beauty, whether it is the breathtaking magnificence of natural phenomena like a mountain range, a tree in mid-autumn, a waterfall, or the formal sculptured appeal of a historical building, a computer model of the double helix of the DNA molecule, or a piece of music by Bach. Confining aesthetic education solely to art lessons would be a diminution of the whole concept of beauty, as well as a missed opportunity.

One reason why some children lose interest in subjects like science at school, only to regain it sometimes as adults, is because spectacular physical phenomena are dealt with in an over-routinised manner. Perhaps it is for fear of losing sight of the vital and often extensive factual information to be learned that prevents some teachers of science from considering not only the beauty of what is being studied, but the moral issues involved in the application of scientific principles, the imagination required to invent and innovate, or the economic and environmental consequences, for good or ill, of different scientific and technological innovations. It ought to be possible to cover both the factual content and some of the related issues, with the latter enhancing, rather than diluting, understanding of the former. It is merely a matter of priority and emphasis. It is perfectly possible to learn correct information about the chemical structure of a crystal and also to appreciate its beauty, or to study a scientific process

Figure 20 Blowing a large bubble – science and beauty

and then reflect on the impact on society of possible positive and negative applications.

An interesting example of the inability of many people to think across subject categories occurs in the field of statistics. One of the problems sometimes faced in modern society is that too few people fully understand quantified data. There are statisticians who understand the techniques they have used, but do not regard it as their duty to look at the implications of what they have deduced, and there are people who say they deplore what they regard as the 'crude' use of statistics, but do not actually understand the procedures that have been employed. A nice piece of irony occurred a few years ago, when university mathematics departments had to lose several hundred posts because of financial cuts. In the committee that was responsible for mathematics in universities someone noticed that the number of posts to be lost was almost exactly the same as the number of mathematics lecturers in the 30 to 40 age bracket. The proposal to solve the problem by dismissing all maths lecturers in their thirties was met with howls of protest from the people who would have been affected, many of whom had previously argued that it was not their responsibility to consider qualitative aspects of the applications of mathematics.

LANGUAGE AND COMMUNICATION

'*Die Grenzen meiner Sprache bedeuten die Grenzen meiner Welt*,' wrote Wittgenstein (1922) in his *Tractatus*. It is a powerful statement, but unless you speak German its power and elegance will elude you. Translated into English, the sentence reads: 'The limits of my language mean (or "indicate") the limits of my world.' This may seem to overemphasise the value and place of language in our lives, but Wittgenstein's assertion, even though he modified his beliefs in later life, can bear closer scrutiny. Without the written and spoken word, and paralinguistic features of communication, like gestures and voice intonation, many of the human functions and transactions we take for granted would not be possible.

Even in the case of severe sensory deprivation, some form of language can effect a remarkable transformation. Many of the children who attend the remarkable school in Zagorsk in Russia, whose methods are inspired by the work of Vygotsky on language and communication, have little or no speech, hearing and sight. Yet by learning the 'language of hands', a communication system fed from person to person by pressing fingers on each other's hands, they are able to achieve a considerable amount, including the discussion of literature and the learning of difficult subject matter and concepts.

It is not only philosophers, however, who have recognised the immense importance of language. Wittgenstein's assertion can also be supported by the study of different languages. When winter comes, most people can use words like 'snow' or 'ice' to describe the weather and landscape. Experts in winter sports may be able to distinguish several types of fresh, slushy or frozen snow, because they ski on it and have use of a range of appropriate terms. But the Lapps have 20 words for 'ice', 11 adjectives meaning 'cold', 41 different words for 'snow' and 26 verbs of freezing and snowing. This rich diversity of expressions allows for a much more fine-grained discrimination and a far deeper understanding of the winter environment than is accessible to those who do not have the relevant vocabulary.

Different languages develop their own conventions which in turn influence both the thoughts and actions of those who speak them. In Balinese the word *paling* represents a state of confusion known to many, but its particular meaning is strongly determined by the cultural environment in which it is used, for its definition is 'the state of trance or drunkenness, or a condition of not knowing where you are, what day it is, where the centre of the island is, not knowing the caste of the person to whom you are speaking'. Such unique concepts are not easy to translate, hence the Italian warning '*Traddutore traditore*,' which means 'to translate is to betray'. Sending well-known expressions through electronic translators from one language to another and then back to the original can soon distort the message. When passed from English to Spanish, German and a few other languages and then finally back to English 'out of sight, out of mind' may return as 'invisible, insane'.

Even in a society which is making more and more use of audio-visual communication, the written and spoken language play a hugely significant part. Written language has been augmented by the increasing use of icons, so that the red or green figures, indicating whether pedestrians must 'stop' or 'go' at traffic lights, have to be just as well-deciphered as the words. Similarly, the numerous international icons indicating danger from high-voltage electricity, radio-active materials or falling rocks, have to be learned, recognised and acted upon with the same accuracy as written warnings. In work, as well as in recreation, home and family life, the ability to read well in a variety of contexts, to write clearly and appropriately, and to speak to different individuals and groups using an appropriate language register remain vital components of an intelligent society. At certain points in history there has been ritualised book burning, an indication of the power of language to influence events, and the fear of those who want to restrict its effects.

There are numerous examples of the importance of language in contemporary life, some of which were cited in Chapter 1. Harrison and Nicoll (1984) have analysed the reading competence needed to cope with the literacy of citizenship. Using measures of text readability they discovered that while tabloid newspapers required the reading capability of the average 12- to 14-year-old, the broadsheet national papers needed a higher competence such as many adults would not have achieved. They also found that, whereas some of the many forms and leaflets that inform citizens of their rights and obligations were written in simple text, at a level of difficulty that secondary pupils of average ability should be able to grasp, others were far more opaque. Yet a number of these more difficult information leaflets were about crucial rights, such as the availability of free spectacles, or the procedures for complaining about inadequate hospital treatment. Those unable to read well would simply miss out on entitlements available to their more literate fellows.

Reading may be important in adult life, but so is the ability to write and speak. Those unable to compose a letter, prepare and present a scientific, technical or commercial report, put together a few pages of continuous prose sustaining an argument or analysing a problem, explain something to a colleague or neighbour, may find that opportunities for further study, prospects for promotion, or even satisfying personal and social relationships, are diminished. Poor grasp of language register, inability to select the best word or the most telling phrase for the context and audience, can sometimes be disastrous. Even so simple a transaction as sending a sick note to school about the absence of one's children requires a grasp of language register. 'I am sorry Caroline and Michael were not at school yesterday, but they both had a bad cold, so I thought it best to keep them at home' is more appropriate than either 'Caroline and her elder sibling were constrained from presenting themselves at your establishment owing to an upper respiratory tract infection' (too pompous), or 'Can I help it if the kids got sick?' (too rude).

In this second dimension of the cubic curriculum, language is one of the most vibrant channels. It seeps into every cranny of the other dimensions, the subject curriculum and teaching and learning strategies. A science teacher explaining Boyle's law to a class of secondary pupils studying physics may state that 'the volume of a given mass of gas at a constant temperature is inversely proportional to its pressure'. This kind of statement can appear overwhelming. It may even be the moment when some pupils decide that physics appears to be full of the kind of abstractions that

THINK BOX 5: LANGUAGE ACROSS THE CURRICULUM

Language is important, but in what sort of experience, what events, what practice or invention do pupils actually participate during the day that might have a positive effect on their language? An observer should follow a class for a period of time, a single lesson, a half or whole day, or a longer period, and attempt to analyse these under various headings:

1 Type of language   What is the balance over types of language activity? How much reading, writing, speaking, listening do groups and individual pupils do during the period of observation?

2 Quality   What is the quality of the language experience? Focusing on one or two individual pupils, concentrate on the content and nature of the reading, writing, speaking, listening, its place in the particular activity, and the extent to which it seems appropriate, however that may be judged.

3 Outcome   This may not be easy to decide, but what seem to be the outcomes of the language activities that are taking place? To what extent do they seem to enhance or inhibit what is being studied?

4 Specific purposes   Look at one specific topic or activity and map out some of the key terms and phrases that must be acquired in order to master it. Check if people are having difficulty with any particular aspect of the language they need.

appeal to future Nobel Prize winners, but not to them. Yet the *concept* of one thing being 'inversely proportional' to another is not an intellectual killer. It is the *language* that causes the problem. If the pupil can realise that 'the more of this – the less of that' is the basic idea, or, expressed in terms of two people seated either side of a seesaw, the higher one person is, the lower the other, wherever they are sitting, then the actual concept is not that elusive.

Language is best learned in a meaningful context. Hence the frequent assertion that, although English teachers take front-line responsibility for nurturing it, every teacher is a language teacher. It is highly unlikely that a science teacher, when explaining Boyle's law, will say that the words 'inversely' and 'proportional' will one day be explained by the class's English teacher, or that it will have to be left to a mathematics lesson. Were that exclusively the case, then life in school would be chaos, beset by myriads of untold and unknown obligations of teachers of different subjects to one another. English lessons in particular would be crammed with the detached and disinterested study of thousands upon thousands of words and phrases which had been stacked up by other teachers in the previous months, like aircraft circling over an airport waiting for a landing slot. Language would become decontextualised and meaningless. In practice, it is more likely that the science teacher will explain the concept 'inversely proportional' in the natural context in which it occurs. But it is also possible that some science teachers, unaware of the importance of language across the curriculum, may ignore the issue completely and merely take it for granted that everyone must have understood what to the teacher is a self-evident piece of vocabulary.

There are many different aspects of language that are relevant to learning. Language *register*, the choosing of the most suitable words and expressions for the audience and context, is one that has already been mentioned. This has considerable relevance not only to the different subjects that may be studied, but to teaching and learning strategies as well, so it will be discussed again in the next chapter when the third dimension of the cubic curriculum is examined. Another feature is the *specialist vocabulary* that each subject uses. Some fields are saturated with long and complex terminology, especially in subjects like medicine, where the labels for parts of the body or illnesses, such as 'medulla oblongata' or 'peritonitis', are often Latin or Greek in origin. In many cases it is difficult, if not impossible, to make progress unless certain key words and expressions are learned. Words like 'area', 'length', 'volume', 'litre', 'metre', 'square' are central taken-for-granted terms in the early stages of the mathematics of measurement. Anyone who does not understand them and cannot use them as part of an everyday active vocabulary would neither grasp the initial stages of measurement, nor be able to progress to higher levels.

Some of these issues are sometimes grouped together under the heading 'language for specific purposes'. Learning about science, technology, religion, history, music, plumbing or gardening, all these draw not only on specialist vocabulary, but on forms of expression that might look out of place or even comical in other contexts. Although using the same grammar and syntax, a technical report on the efficiency of a car engine would not usually be written in exactly the same language as a poem or a critique of a piece of music, though in classical times, Greek mathematicians and scientists, like Euclid and Archimedes, wrote their texts in verse. Nowadays, however, a phrase like 'the torque generated by the twin spark engine' clearly comes from a technical report, whereas 'the pathos of the final scene provoked deep emotion from the audience' occurred in a theatre critique, and 'I look forward to seeing you next Tuesday' is the language of letter writing.

Since language lies so close to the heart of learning, it is vital that teachers are not only aware of the issues and principles involved, but that there is deliberate scrutiny of the extent to which children are acquiring, or being confused by, the language they need in particular circumstances. It is also an issue for schools to consider on both an individual and group basis, in that the school's 'language climate' – that is, the extent to which all teachers encourage language development – is important, but so is the experience of individual students. It is possible that some pupils enjoy a rich language experience, while others, even those in the same class, may not. Think Box 5 focuses on both the group and individual perspective.

THINKING

Language and thought are closely linked. Thinking is often silent language, talking to oneself, so our language is bound to exert an influence on our thought. Some children, especially young ones, will even talk aloud when they are thinking about an issue. Images also play a strong part in thought, and most of us can conjure up a mental picture of faces, locations or abstract shapes to which we might not consciously give a verbal label. Developing the ability to think in different fields like mathematics, history or science, to recall information when needed, to solve problems, to analyse critically, all these are vital elements of education which ripple across subject boundaries and teaching strategies.

There are many different ways of classifying how we think. In education there is often greatest stress on the acquisition of concepts. Small children soon learn to recognise simple figures, like a triangle or a square. Before long they have a rudimentary concept of 'geometric shape', even though they would not normally use that term. As they grow older they acquire many more concepts in different subjects, like 'mammal', 'the past', 'sentence' or 'musical note'. They also learn social concepts such as 'rules', 'tidiness' and 'sharing'. Older pupils will learn to cope with more complex concepts such as 'photosynthesis', 'democracy' or 'probability'.

As was pointed out earlier, in a rapidly changing environment the ability to think in different ways is essential, as is the understanding of key organising concepts in the various subjects, seen as a major goal in most classrooms. Some educationists, like Bloom (1956) and Taba (1971), have seen thinking as a hierarchy in which the simplest level is the recall of information. Above that comes what is sometimes called 'higher-order' thinking, where the learner has to do more than remember facts by going on to use them in some way, like grouping and labelling, predicting, making inferences, establishing generalisations, evaluating, problem solving, or speculating. The terms 'lower' and 'higher' can be confusing here, because the so-called 'lower-order' thinking involved in factual recall may be more exacting than some supposedly 'higher-order' inferring. Being able to recall the formula of DNA is much more complex than making the inference, when visiting a friend and finding a 'Gone fishing' sign on the door, that he is not at home.

To take an earlier example as an illustration of this view of categories of thought, consider children learning about the genus 'Insects'. According to the hierarchical approach to classifying children's thinking, the simplest level would be *recalling factual information*, such as that insects have six legs, antennae, wings, three parts to their body. The next level up would be *labelling* and *grouping*, often important elements in the understanding of key concepts. In learning to understand what insects are, 'labelling' might involve thinking about, and being able to attach labels to, the parts of the body known as the 'thorax' or the 'abdomen'. In the case of 'grouping', pupils would need to be able to work out, from known characteristics, that flies, bees and wasps are 'insects', whereas spiders and scorpions are 'arachnids'.

Advanced skill in thinking generally, and understanding concepts in particular, is often revealed if someone can *evaluate* or *make inferences*, as this requires the recall

Figure 21   Learning mathematics concepts, such as 'shape' and 'space', as well as social
concepts such as 'rules' and 'sharing'
Source: Introduction to Classroom Observation, E.C. Wragg, Routledge, 1994

of information followed by an act of rational judgement. 'How insects fit into their environment' is an aspect of the topic that should evoke this kind of thinking. In the last chapter I raised the issue of children's intuitive thinking, which may sometimes mislead, but can also lead to flashes of insight. When this happens there is often a neat link between language and thought, as children, lacking the necessary technical vocabulary, use natural language and everyday direct experience to express their thoughts. One 8-year-old child, observed studying insects during one of our research projects (Wragg 1993), was asked by his teacher to talk about the insect's antennae:

Teacher:	(*pointing*) What are these?
Pupil:	Feelers.
Teacher:	And what are they for?
Pupil:	Tasting the air.
Teacher:	Yes, 'tasting the air', that's a good description.

Sometimes higher levels of thinking need to be reached step by step, rather than in one single leap. Studying the history of the United Nations, for example, might involve first recalling and then weighing up the evidence about the role of the League of Nations after the First World War. This could then be compared with what is known about the performance of the United Nations since the Second World War, in order to decide whether the United Nations has made an effective contribution to resolving conflicts between different countries.

Problem solving, prediction and speculative thinking

These require not only the ability to recall, infer and evaluate, but also to make a leap of the imagination. In order to decide how best to resolve what appears to be a deadlock, or what to do when faced with a moral dilemma, the student has to solve a problem. Anyone wishing to forecast the likely weather for the following day must be able to use available evidence to predict forthcoming events on the basis of preceding ones. Speculating and hypothesising involve making an intelligent and informed guess about the reasons why something has occurred, or about what might ensue in future. This demands several types of thinking, including the recall of information, the evaluation of evidence and subsequently, as with problem solving and predicting, a leap into the unknown. 'Imagination', the ability to engage in unusual or novel thinking, or to picture in the mind, could be seen as a subset of the cube channel 'thought', but I have given it a separate label in the second dimension, as it is worth considering in its own right, in certain circumstances.

To look down the 'thought' channel of the second dimension of the cubic curriculum invites reflection and action on a number of matters. Some of these relate to teaching and learning strategies, like the need to remember key pieces of information, so I shall return to those in Chapter 5 when the third dimension is discussed, but others concern the first dimension of the cube. The question arises, for example, whether there are specific forms of thinking that are unique to, or are best nurtured in, particular subject disciplines. Is 'scientific thinking' completely different from 'historical thinking' or 'musical thinking'? Like many of the most intriguing human riddles, this question has more than one answer.

On the surface there appears to be much in common. All subjects embrace a body of factual knowledge, at its simplest level the names of key constituents and concepts, such as 'atom', 'treaty', 'semi-quaver', 'rectangle', which will inform and shape people's thinking when studying the discipline. In some subjects these key concepts are more ordered, sequenced and uncontentious, whereas in others they may be more diffuse, ill-defined and problematic. There is not too much argument about what a 'parallelogram' is, but less agreement about what is 'fair', or what constitutes 'quality'.

It also appears, at first glance, that many types of thinking are common to all subjects. 'Evaluation' can take place when someone is appraising the outcome of a scientific experiment or reflecting on the merits of an urban development or a symphony. 'Prediction' occurs not only when someone conducting a scientific experiment makes an intelligent and informed guess about the result of it, but also when a musician anticipates the likely next note of a melody, or a painter has an understanding of the probable results on canvas of mixing two or more coloured paints. 'Making inferences', 'speculating', 'imagining' are all types of thinking that can appear in different subject contexts.

This does not, however, mean that there is nothing specific about thinking in different contexts, only generalities. Nor is there a guarantee of automatic transfer from one subject to the next of any particular thinking expertise. Someone able to draw brilliant and incisive conclusions from complex scientific data may be quite unable to make an inference about the different harmonies that might be added to a musical melody, or may have few insights into the intricacies of human behaviour. Whatever *potential* or *prior experience* students may have, when they first start learning in a new field, it is education that offers the *opportunity* for engaging in the different forms of thinking that are relevant to the subject. It is logical, therefore, to offer pupils the maximum chances to develop the range and quality of their thinking in all the subjects that they learn.

This raises the question whether 'thinking' should be taught in its own right, either as a subject in the first dimension of the cube, or as an identifiable component of each subject. There are several possibilities already in existence. Even quite young children, when studying science, can learn to think scientifically: to hypothesise, control different variables, record results, reflect on findings. They are likely to use natural language like 'make a guess', 'carry out a fair test', but appropriate rigour is possible.

There have been numerous proposals to teach specific thinking skills, sometimes in specific subjects, on other occasions in a more general way. General programmes have sometimes concentrated on developing skill at problem solving or creative thinking, by getting pupils to think in unusual ways and look for off-beat solutions. The work of Vygotsky (1978) and Feuerstein (1980) helps children explore and discuss different thinking strategies, but not in any particular subject context, part of the argument being that children may already have failed in these subjects, so they may need a fresh start, free from associations of failure. One problem with this approach is that pupils may not find it easy to transfer these free-floating strategies to their various school subjects.

By contrast, Shayer (1996) worked specifically in the field of science. He found that, when trained systematically to understand scientific thinking, children did better in national tests of science and mathematics. Taba (1971) argued that, if taught how to think in different categories, children of quite modest ability, when studying historical topics, like 'The Pioneers', could operate at a higher level of thought. She produced teaching modules showing how teachers could move on from information recall to grouping, labelling, predicting, making inferences and generalisations. There are stories in a reading scheme for 8- and 9-year-olds (Wragg 1996) in which the central characters, and thus the reader, have to learn how to think in different ways in order to solve problems in various contexts.

In addition, there have been proposals that 'thinking' should be a taught subject in its own right, which would put it in the first dimension of the cube. Lipman (1991) has sponsored a move to introduce the teaching of philosophy in schools, to make children think about philosophical issues. Whether thinking is seen as being principally in the first or second dimension of the cube is a matter of individual taste, but there is little argument that it should be somewhere in the curriculum, and many of the issues raised above about language in the curriculum apply in the case of thinking as well. Indeed, it is a topic I shall return to in Chapters 5 and 6 when I look in more detail at teaching and learning.

PERSONAL AND SOCIAL DEVELOPMENT AND CITIZENSHIP

At the beginning of this book I described how, in the rapidly changing work and social environment of the twenty-first century, it will be important for citizens to have considerable personal qualities and traits, such as imagination, determination, flexibility, and a willingness to learn throughout their life. Such aspirations run along two channels of the second dimension of the cubic curriculum, labelled 'personal' and 'social'. The second of these might also be called 'citizenship', so both items have been used. Some of these aspirations have already been discussed, but others, like determination and flexibility, are individual characteristics which must be nurtured if people are to be drivers of their own destiny, rather than mere passengers who always need to be steered by others. Achieving personal autonomy, as well as enjoying harmonious membership of a team, are aspirations that can easily come into conflict with each other, but they are characteristics of a mature citizenry. They are noble hopes which have enticed and frustrated countless generations.

At this point the argument can easily be overwhelmed by considerations about the extent to which members of society have any control at all over their own future. Those who reject the notion of free will may argue that we are in any case at the mercy of forces beyond our control which may have been pre-determined, so this negates the element of choice in the matter. I reject this view on the grounds that, if we in fact have no choice, there is no point in pretending that we do, but on the other hand if we *are* able to make autonomous choices, I would prefer people to be active and positive, rather than acquiescent and resigned.

The curriculum can enhance or inhibit opportunities to acquire independence of mind and develop personal characteristics. Looking down the 'personal' channel of the second dimension and across the first dimension of the cube, one can see how children might develop flexibility, as opposed to rigidity. The ability to adapt, to continue learning, to adjust what one has learned to novel situations, all these were mentioned above as key elements of surviving and prospering in a rapidly changing society. Are students encouraged to keep an open mind? Is their curiosity stimulated or anaesthetised? Do they develop adaptive routines and flourish, or are they intellectual dinosaurs who try to muddle along on what has stood them in good stead before, whether appropriate to new circumstances or not? These are among many questions one can ask when looking down the second dimension at the first dimension of the cubic curriculum.

Many other personal characteristics can be studied by looking down the 'personal' and 'social/citizenship' channels of the second dimension. In a subject like design and

'Now for the hard puzzle,' said Max.
He opened the puzzle and read it to us.

> You got the wood,
> So that was good.
> Now can you see
> How to get the key.

Yes, Castle Thinkadink was getting harder! We all thought hard.

'I've got it!' shouted Max. 'We use the plank to get across the pit!'

'How will that help us get the key?' said Vicky.

'We take the boxes across the plank, climb on the boxes and get the key!'

Figure 22 Young children learn about thinking and how to solve problems

Source: Billy's Guide to Thinking, an information book, 1996, Ted Wragg, *In Flight* Reading Scheme, Nelson

technology, students' personal development might be nurtured if they are able to use their initiative as they plan something, and show determination to see it through, even if working against the odds. Willingness to take personal responsibility for, and eventually pride in the quality of what is produced would also be promoted. The same would apply to writing an essay in an English lesson, performing a movement in a dance class, researching a project in the library or taking photographs of a school trip. The aim is close to that described by the German writer Friedrich Schiller, who spoke of becoming a '*schöne Seele*', a beautiful soul – that is, doing something, however modest, to the best of one's ability.

This is both an individual and a group matter. If the 'personal' channel is the one that focuses on the singular, then the 'social/citizenship' channel concentrates on the plural, for it is when individuals are able to pool and share their virtues that social development takes place and the whole community benefits. Studying the curriculum to see what opportunities it offers for both personal and social development can highlight subjects like drama, in which pupils may explore their own values, beliefs and behaviour, as well as that of others, through role play, improvisation and the enactment of different kinds of plays. Literary studies in pupils' native or a foreign language may serve the same purpose. Subjects like history, geography and religious education offer the possibility of studying the behaviour of individuals and groups in a variety of settings, both in the past and the present. There is no guarantee, however, that knowledge of virtuous and shameful behaviour by others will in itself produce personal and social behaviour of a high standard by the pupil. There are many examples throughout history of well-educated tyrants.

This raises a number of related questions about personal and social education. One is the extent to which teachers should teach explicitly absolute moral values. The character Fagin in Charles Dickens' novel *Oliver Twist* is an example of someone, albeit fictitious, who was in one sense an 'effective' teacher, in that he successfully imparted what he intended to teach, but who would be condemned as abhorrent by most people for teaching children to steal – something that is a criminal offence. As public servants preparing people for a harmonious society, teachers must, in general, support the law of the land. The dilemma comes when questions of 'right' and 'wrong' are not so clear cut. While there is little ambiguity about some laws, there is not always universal agreement in a society about others, and those that seem unfair are often changed.

The study of different societies will often highlight a variety of practices. What is permissible in one may be illegal in another. Pupils will learn that it was legal for young children to work in factories during the nineteenth century, but illegal during the twentieth century. A society may condemn the taking of a person's life as unlawful on most occasions, but then condone it during a war. Divorce is acceptable in some communities but not in others. Hence the interest, in lessons specifically set aside for personal, social and moral education, in exploring the consequences of different actions over moral issues. An example is: 'You discover one evening that your best friend has tried an illegal drug. Do you report him to the police, tell his parents, tell a teacher, suggest he confesses, discuss the matter with him, ignore it, take some other

Figure 23   Personal development – students learn to take responsibility for and pride in the
quality of their work
(*Photo courtesy of Exeter College*)

course of action?' Teachers are sometimes in an exposed position here, as their own
views may not be the same as those of a pupil's parents, for example, and, however
disarming teachers may be about the importance of their own personal views,
members of a class will frequently ask them what they themselves think. It is then a
personal decision how frank to be in the circumstances, though it should be discussed
at staff meetings when policies and procedures are decided.

Another important point about personal and social development is that it is
fostered not only inside, but also outside the classroom. The law regards teachers
as being *in loco parentis* – that is, acting as a sensible parent would, throughout

the school day, in the playgrounds and corridors, as well as in the classrooms, workshops, laboratories and on the playing fields. Teachers have what the law calls the 'duty of care', and they can be sued for negligence if they ignore accidents or fail to protect their students' welfare. Looking down the 'personal' and 'social/ citizenship' channels affords a good opportunity to see how the whole of school life is influencing pupils' personal and social development. Pious lessons on rights and wrongs and care for others are wasted if pupils are allowed to bully one another in the playground, or if they destroy one another's confidence during team games or group projects. Becoming both a capable individual person and a good citizen is not something that is only nurtured in lessons labelled 'citizenship' or 'personal, social and moral development'.

OTHER CHANNELS IN THE SECOND DIMENSION

Numerous other labels could be added to the second dimension of the cubic curriculum, for many issues straddle the subjects being taught and the methods of teaching and learning being employed. Indeed, in the field of vocational development in particular, these overarching matters of personal development are frequently incorporated into profiles of candidates for awards, qualifications and job appointments. *Numeracy* is a good example of another domain which could be seen entirely as something taught in mathematics classes, a first-dimension issue, or as a genuinely cross-curricular matter. After all, there are quantitative approaches in many subjects, and understanding number, handling numerical operations accurately and confidently, applying mathematics in a variety of work and leisure activities are all regarded as desirable. Scientists and social scientists make a great deal of use of number. Much of geography can involve quantification, and even traditional arts subjects, like history, sometimes employ quantitative methods.

Aesthetic development is another important area, as was mentioned at the beginning of this chapter, when the argument was put forward that it was not only in the arts that beauty might be appreciated, but also in science, history, geography, mathematics, a whole range of scheduled subjects, as well as in the whole environment of the school. When the 900th anniversary of the Domesday Book was celebrated in 1986 I wanted to make sure that the aesthetic dimension was not ignored, so I worked with a class of 8- to 11-year-olds in a small village primary school to re-enact the scene when the Domesday commissioners came to their village. The most important focus was on the historical aspect, why the Domesday Book was compiled by King William and what it actually was. The village actually had an entry in the Domesday Book as well as a Norman church, so we were able to act out the visit of the commissioners in a realistic and authentic way. All the children had Norman-style clothes made from discarded fabrics. They paraded into the church in the presence of their parents and members of the community to perform their version of the historical event. As they entered, a Gregorian chant echoed round the ancient church. It was an awe-inspiring atmosphere in which the learning of eleventh-century British history was the central

THINK BOX 6: PERSONAL EDUCATION AND CITIZENSHIP

- -

Looking across the first dimension of the cubic curriculum and at the whole school, what opportunities are there for personal and social development?

1   Subjects   What subject content and activities appear to foster personal and social development? Look at different subjects to see what impact they appear to have on helping pupils mature into good citizens of the twenty-first century, and how they affect their values and beliefs.

2   School ethos   What effect does the whole school have on pupils? Consider behaviour in the school playground, on corridors and places where people meet and circulate. What is the effect of the physical environment, and can it be improved?

3   Dilemmas   What do teachers do when faced with dilemmas over personal and social issues? Discuss the similarities and differences in viewpoint among teachers on the same staff about, for example, the extent to which they would want to state their own views on personal, social and moral issues that occur in discussion.

4   Negative effects   It is not easy to do this in an honest and subtle way, but try to evaluate any negative effects the school might have on personal and social development. Although it is customary to argue that everything is being done to nurture positive behaviour and values, are there any examples of children's personal development being inhibited or suppressed, or of negative social behaviour being condoned, even if unintentionally?

purpose, but the clothing, the drama, the music and the church architecture added an important aesthetic dimension.

A further cross-curricular matter is the whole question of political education. Like other second-dimension notions this could be in the first dimension, for 'politics' is a perfectly legitimate scheduled subject on the timetable. However, politics is about the use of power, the ability to control and determine the behaviour of others, and there are numerous direct and oblique messages about the use of power in any society both inside and outside the classroom. As with the cross-curricular issues described above, political education can take place in history lessons, when the uses and misuses of power will be studied, and in geography, especially urban geography, which looks at

Figure 24   Children re-enact the 1086 visit of the Domesday commissioners in this Norman village church

decisions over resources, locations of amenities and decision making about the environment. It can occur in other subjects too, and it can also feature in school life generally, in the classroom, when pupils may or may not be consulted about the programme of work and its implementation, and in the whole school.

In general, pupils have relatively little direct power, as most of the decisions about curriculum, rules, programmes, buildings and facilities tend to be made by the head, teachers and governors. They do, however, have some power at the micro-level. In many classrooms certain decisions about choice, types of activity, the following of instructions may be negotiated, or interpreted flexibly, rather than imposed unilaterally. It is worth reviewing the decisions that pupils are able to make about their own learning, not because some omni-purpose 'ideal' balance exists between teachers' decisions and those made by pupils, but rather because learning both to follow instructions and also to make autonomous judgements are important elements of growing up. Power is an inescapable feature of both children's and adults' lives. How to respond to it, and also how to exercise it judiciously if one has it, are part of every citizen's day-to-day responsibilities.

CHAPTER FIVE

Teaching and Learning Styles, the Third Dimension

The third dimension of the cubic curriculum, like the other two dimensions before it, covers enormous fields, for both teaching and learning have a huge literature written about them. The argument was put forward in Chapters 1 and 2 that if children now in school are to continue learning with enthusiasm for several decades after they have left full-time education, then the means by which they learn and are taught in the first phase of their lives will exert considerable influence on the later stages of it. That is why teaching and learning should be important integral elements of the curriculum, rather than a detached afterthought to it, and hence why they constitute the crucial third dimension of the cubic curriculum model.

For reasons explained earlier, the model of the cube, in order to be both manageable and drawn in perspective, has to be foreshortened in the third dimension. This prevents the showing of many of the labels and categories which could be displayed, so only a brief selection from the myriads of possibilities can be shown. The analysis of teaching and learning in a book of this scope will have to be much more concise than I would like, but I have written more fully on these topics elsewhere (Wragg 1984, 1993, 1994; Wragg and Brown 1993; Brown and Wragg 1993). Teaching and learning need to be seen together, but it is worth considering them under separate headings, despite their interdependence, so that the one can be examined in more detail, while the other is in the background in softer focus. If pupils really are to be assiduous and effective learners throughout the several decades after the initial phase of their education, then the foundations of learning are crucial, so I shall start with them.

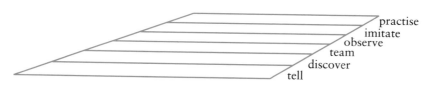

Figure 25   The third dimension – teaching and learning styles

LEARNING

There are many aspects of learning that are common to all or most learners, but there are also significant differences between them. Intelligence, personality, maturity, environment, emotions, motivation, all these are influential on learning, but in different ways for different people. Someone who is intelligent, but lazy, immature and unmotivated may learn less than another person who starts with an apparently lower mental ability, but manifests more purpose, drive and determination. Certain people can become so frustrated and emotional about learning a particular subject, concept or skill that they set up an emotional blockage to it which forms a barrier to progress, whereas others are able to tolerate frustration more readily, so the obstacles to improvement are minimised.

Several aspects of learning have been regularly identified as important, including the ones below. Inevitably these descriptions of factors influencing how children and adults learn relate closely to the first two major dimensions of the cube, subjects and cross-curricular notions, and to teaching as well as to learning. This stresses once more that the curriculum must be seen as an organic whole, even though it is possible to divide it into constituent parts for analysis and scrutiny.

Familiarity

Learning can be made more effective if it is related to what is familiar. We often feel least at ease with fresh material that is alien and completely novel. The assertion 'Size can vary. Jibjabs are leontini, and so are gibblegobbles' makes little sense to us, whereas 'Size can vary. Eagles are birds, and so are sparrows' is easily recognised as a statement about a larger and smaller member of the same class. That is why teachers often try to establish a bridge or a link with something familiar, making use of an illustrative example or an analogy. In the study cited earlier of how teachers taught the topic 'insects' to children aged 8 and 9 (Wragg 1993) it was found that some explained features like an insect's eye by using language, or selecting analogies, which would be familiar to children of that age, likening it to 'a plastic bag full of marbles' or 'a bank of television sets'.

Association

Concepts that appear to float freely, detached from anything on which to hang them, may be difficult to remember. Being able to make associations, especially ones that seize attention, or even that are strikingly unusual, can sometimes help with new learning, or with the recall of what appears to be half forgotten. That is why some of the standard approaches for helping people to learn or remember, nowadays often sold through newspaper adverts although they have been well known for centuries, make use of bizarre visual association.

One such technique is to learn a set of words that rhyme with numbers, like 'three – tree', or 'ten – hen' and then make a visual association between what is to be learned and one of the rhyming objects. Thus if the names of 10 musical instruments had to be memorised, the learner would visualise as vividly as possible the relevant association. If the third instrument in the list were 'violin', then recalling the rhyme 'three – tree' would produce a picture of a violin wedged up a tree. If musical instrument number ten ('hen') were a piano, then the learner would visualise a hen sitting on a piano. Association is so powerful in learning, that a smell, an image, even the mere mention of one single word, can bring to mind several other associated ideas. Mention of the city name 'Dallas' immediately evokes vivid associations – with oil production, a widely shown television series, an American football team or the assassination of President Kennedy.

Transfer

The related ideas of 'transfer' and 'interference' were discussed above in Chapter 3. One of the great expectations of any curriculum, especially in the light of the points made earlier about education for a very long future, is that what is learned will not only be valuable in its own right, but will also allow the bearer of knowledge and skills to use these in varying, or even entirely novel, circumstances. It is what Gilbert Ryle (1949), in his book *States of Mind*, called the difference between 'knowing *that*' and 'knowing *how*'. In other words, for effective transfer to take place, it is usually necessary to understand the inner nature of what has been learned, to be inside the principles involved, not merely to be able to repeat the external labels. Car mechanics who actually understand how a car functions will usually be able to repair a vehicle they have not seen before, because they should have a general grasp of how a car's engine, brakes or fuel system actually work. They can then transfer their knowledge and skill to the new vehicle, because they understand and recognise the workings of its key components. Someone who had no idea of how a car works would have to operate at a 'programmed' level and would be lost on encountering anything unexpected or beyond the detailed instructions.

The evidence on transfer is mixed (Gage and Berliner 1984), but it does seem that, in addition to understanding key principles, it may be important for the learner to have some true-to-life practice in order to make the transfer of knowledge and skills effective. Being able to throw a ball accurately with your right hand does not ensure that you can automatically do as well with your left hand, but practising left-handed throws should aid the transfer to the less accurate arm of some of the skilful hand-eye co-ordination that has been acquired with the natural throwing arm. 'Interference' is the obverse of transfer. Instead of the learner being helped by prior knowledge or skill of a similar kind, these may instead act as a distracter, getting in the way of learning. Transfer and interference are of particular importance in considering the curriculum in this multi-dimensional way. It cannot be assumed that knowledge of one subject will automatically help with another, though it may.

The topics raised in the different sections of this book are closely interlinked, and once again the matter of children's intuitive understanding is relevant. When facilitating transfer through giving pupils practice, teachers need to ensure that interference is not occurring, as this can lead to the learning of misconceptions and errors. Two examples, both connected with eggs, show some of the problems when children have an incorrect intuition and so make wrong assumptions on the basis of prior learning. A pupil, when asked how we can tell whether water is hard or soft, replied that the answer could be discovered by boiling an egg: if it was hard boiled then the water must be hard, and if it was soft boiled the water would be soft. The notion of 'hardness' and 'softness' in one context had been wrongly transferred to another. In the second instance a child was asked to locate the embryo inside a chicken's egg. He pointed to the whole of the yolk. His knowledge of a baby chicken being yellow led him to a wrong conclusion based on colour and size, rather than on a proper understanding of origin and growth. Prior knowledge can transfer correctly, or mislead on occasion.

Observation

The ability of children to observe, and subsequently to imitate, can be quite remarkable. The term 'observation' is intended here not to mean exclusively using one's eyes. All the senses can be involved – hearing, touch, taste and smell, as well as seeing – so that children gain greater familiarity with and understanding of what surrounds them. Language development is a good example of how even very young children can learn to listen to, and then mimic, the sounds they hear around them. Quite early in their lives, at only a few months or a year, babies will babble 'echolalia' like 'ma ma, ba ba, fa fa, da da, za za, dem dem, ga ga, va va', repeating their own version of the syllables and words they hear from others, no matter what language is being spoken.

But the senses can also deceive, and an important part of the curriculum should be learning to use them with discrimination. In their science lessons children should one day learn that a stick placed in water is not bent, as the eyes suggest, but rather that the light from it is refracted in the water, because its speed changes when it passes from one substance (water) to another (air). In their language or music lessons children should be encouraged to listen sharply, so they learn that a particular sound in a foreign language is not exactly the same as a similar one in their native tongue, or that the sound made by one musical instrument is different from that made by another. In art classes they should be given opportunities to look carefully at the vast range of shapes, textures, colours and shades that surround them, so that they are aware of these when they create their drawings, paintings or sculptures. *Observation with discrimination* is a vital part of the cubic curriculum and an essential preparation for adult life. Important decisions throughout life are often made on the basis of observed phenomena, events and behaviour, so it is better that these are accurately rather than inaccurately witnessed.

Figure 26   Learning to observe from an early age

Imitation

Observation and imitation lie at the heart of the drive that pushes children to attain competence in several fields. Nurturing rather than repressing that drive should be a central purpose of the curriculum. As was the case with observation, however, uncritical imitation can also lead learners astray. Learning by imitation is sometimes called, in vocational courses, 'sitting by Nellie', where 'Nellie' is deemed to be the archetypal competent 'old hand' who has mastered the skills the trainee is supposed to be learning. What is crucial, however, is the nature and quality of the model being copied. Nellie may be ill informed, not especially competent or hopelessly out of date.

The field of domestic plumbing offers an interesting example here. In the United Kingdom for many years it has been customary, when installing a shower, to take the water from the pipe containing the hot feed. As this usually comes at lower pressure than the mains cold water supply, the result is often a weak flow from the shower head, and alternate freezing and scalding water from any mixer taps when someone in another room uses water from the supply. Yet in many other countries it has been common practice for years to plumb the shower into the cold feed, thereby diminishing these problems. Nellie may well not know of practice elsewhere. Too much reliance on imitation alone as a form of learning can be too conservative, merely propagating the *status quo*, rather than improving skill and knowledge. Over a period of years the constant imitation of poor models would reduce the quality of performance in a subject or profession.

The same strictures apply to the imitation of models that are not just dated, but palpably wrong. Hence the caution needed when pupils are asked to demonstrate a particular skill or respond to a question. It is commonplace and quite legitimate for pupils, as well as the teacher, to show others how to do something – for example, to carry out a gymnastic movement, or sing a melody in a music lesson. There are distinct advantages to offering models by peers, showing what is attainable, rather than overawing learners with an expert demonstration, but there needs to be scrutiny of the quality and frequency of such models.

I often teach foreign languages to secondary school pupils and adults. Sometimes they have been taught by a previous teacher who had poor pronunciation and intonation and have faithfully copied incorrect forms of the language. In these circumstances I find it very difficult to get them to re-learn a correct version of the language when they have spent so long imitating wrong models. Indeed, those who are specially good at learning through imitation will be just as competent at learning errors as correct forms, and children with a good visual or auditory memory will see or hear clearly in their head the mistakes they have witnessed, and repeat them later.

Unpicking patterns that have been firmly laid down in the brain can be devilishly difficult, especially if incorrect or undesired forms have been rehearsed and repeated many times. In such circumstances, 'unlearning' is far harder than learning. If a teacher demonstrates a science experiment in an unsafe manner, for example, many pupils will simply copy it, for they usually, certainly in the early stages of schooling, possess no other models that offer comparison. The strong belief that pupils may use teachers and other pupils as models has been well established for many years. Many years ago Anderson (1939) found that young children in pre-school classes appeared to copy the predominant behaviour of their teachers, and in those classes where the teacher was more dominative, the children were more likely to be over-assertive, snatching toys, or ordering others around, whereas in more 'integrative' classes they were more likely to share toys and wait their turn. Much later Bandura (1977) argued that imitation occurred not only when children actually witnessed the behaviour of others, but sometimes when they heard or read about it. This puts considerable pressure on teachers to be both good models for their pupils' learning of knowledge and skills in the subjects of the curriculum, as well as to exert a positive influence on their social behaviour by their own conduct.

Emotions

There is a close connection between emotion and motivation, but there are also separate issues to be considered. Emotional states can exert a powerful influence on what is learned, or conversely act as a barrier to learning. Emotions express the language and intelligence of feelings as disparate as joy, grief, anger or fear. They can be separate from one another or intertwined, sadness tinged with anger, fear saturated with excitement, happiness tainted by regret.

Emotional states that, on the surface, appear to be different, can actually be accompanied by similar physical symptoms. Anger and excitement are forms of arousal that usually go with raised heart and blood-pressure rates. Both may either help or hinder learning, depending on whether they are under control and managed effectively, or beyond restraint. Anger or excitement may result in determined efforts to reach one's goal, but uncontrolled anger or excitement can produce aimless energy, and eventually frustration and poor performance. This applies especially in novel situations.

Pupils studying mathematics who meet algebra for the first time may rise to the challenge of coping with letters instead of the more familiar numbers, and this may produce a sense of exhilaration and achievement. Others, however, will become angry and aggressive at their inability to understand immediately and frustration may result, with a subsequent psychological blockage towards algebra in particular, and possibly mathematics in general.

For some people encountering novelty produces a state of anxiety, and anxiety is another emotional state that can influence learning for good or ill. As is the case with other emotions, a certain amount of it can be positive, but too much or too little may have a negative effect. If we showed too little anxiety when crossing the road, we would be knocked over, for we would not even bother to look around for danger. Too much anxiety, however, and we would never leave home for fear of an accident. Examination candidates with no anxiety might not bother to revise or do their best on the day, whereas those beset by anxiety may panic, find they cannot concentrate, become paralysed with their own fear, and thus underperform.

Emotional states are an important part of the curriculum for many reasons. It could be argued that emotional development should be a subject on the curriculum, a topic worth studying in its own right, and therefore more legitimately located in the first dimension of the cubic curriculum. That is a tenable point of view, as is the argument that it should figure in the second dimension as a cross-curricular issue, for pupils' emotions may be scrutinised and fostered in numerous subjects, especially, though not exclusively, in the arts. It is included in the third dimension principally because it is such an important element of teaching and learning, one that should be important to people throughout their lives, and something therefore that pupils and teachers must understand, and teachers in particular need to help with during difficult moments when motivation has flagged. In positive form emotions offer a stimulation and enhancement to pupils' learning, in negative form they can be a killer of it. I once supervised a PhD student who was in tears of frustration and wanted to pack in her research in the early stages, because she could not understand fully one of the statistical techniques she needed to use. Fortunately she persisted and completed a very good thesis.

Motivation

The term 'motivation' is part of everyday discourse about learning, both in professional and lay circles. A reasonably well-educated parent or pupil is just as likely to talk about motivation, or lack of it, as a teacher or an educational psychologist. Closely linked to what was said about emotional states in the previous section, motivation can fluctuate from time to time, even within the same individual. Few people would say that the nature and intensity of their motivation to learn something is identical every single day of their lives, partly because motivation consists of a number of related components, all of which are important, but some of which are highly significant for the curriculum.

Two of the most important of these are *time* and *arousal*. Someone who is motivated will simply spend more time on a topic and be in a greater state of arousal than someone else who is not. Imagine looking through a daily newspaper during a week in which the world chess championship is being played. Each day there is a column in the newspaper, written by the paper's chess expert, showing the latest game in the series, with a list of all the moves and a diagram of the chess board at a crucial point in the game. If you are unmotivated in the field of chess, then each day your eye passes blindly across the page with the game on it, not even registering, consciously at any rate, that such a column exists. If you are slightly motivated, you may confine yourself to a swift glance at the match score and a cursory read of the report. Should you be moderately well motivated, you may read through the report, then take out a chess set and spend a few minutes playing through the game reported that day.

At the highest level of motivation, however, someone so highly motivated as to justify the label 'fanatic' would cut out the column, take it down to the local chess club, argue into the early hours with fellow enthusiasts about the merits or otherwise of each move, and eventually file away the excised cutting with others, returning every so often to re-play and think about the game in question. So far as 'motivation' is concerned, the difference between the 'fanatic', the 'interested' and the 'indifferent', in terms of the amount of time devoted to the topic, and the degree of emotional arousal, could be enormous. Though there is not a perfect correlation between time, arousal and learning, it is hardly surprising that highly motivated students usually learn more than the marginally keen.

In itself 'time' is an empty concept. Time can be spent copying out telephone directories, so the mere assignment of a portion of it to a subject or activity will not guarantee that what is done is worth while. Yet *how* time is spent, both by teachers and pupils, is a perfectly legitimate concern when looking at the curriculum. Similarly, the notion of 'arousal' does not mean a great deal out of context, for it could be destructive or inimical to learning, the manifestation of anger, an unfocused state of excitement, frustration even.

Looking at the degree of attentiveness that children bring to their work, however, is certainly of concern. Learning to concentrate, to be persistent, to puzzle something out, to step back and start again if bemused or frustrated, are all important lessons for lifelong learning, whether in structured groups or as an autonomous adult. The

KEENE on CHESS

BY RAYMOND KEENE
CHESS CORRESPONDENT

Elite review

Today I continue my review of elite tournaments of the past which might challenge the Las Palmas event, starting on December 8, for the accolade for strongest tournament of all time.

Having dominated his rivals at the two great tournaments of 1895-96 and St Petersburg 1914, the amazing Emanuel Lasker, then 55 years old, also took clear first at New York in 1924. As at St Petersburg ten years earlier, he again outdistanced Capablanca, Alekhine and Marshall, as well as other star players such as Reti, Maroczy, Bogolyubov and Tartakower. In the following game the great Alekhine is strategically outgunned at every stage.

White: Alexander Alekhine
Black: Emanuel Lasker
New York 1924

Queen's Gambit Declined

1	d4	d5
2	c4	e6
3	Nf3	Nf6
4	Nc3	Nbd7
5	cxd5	exd5
6	Bf4	c6
7	e3	Nh5
8	Bd3	Nxf4
9	exf4	Bd6
10	g3	0-0
11	0-0	Re8
12	Qc2	Nf8
13	Nd1	f6
14	Ne3	Be6
15	Nh4	Bc7
16	b4	Bb6
17	Nf3	Bf7
18	b5	Bh5
19	g4	Bf7
20	bxc6	Rc8
21	Qb2	bxc6
22	f5	Qd6
23	Ng2	Bc7
24	Rfe1	h5
25	h3	Nh7
26	Rxe8+	Rxe8
27	Re1	Rb8
28	Qc1	Ng5
29	Ne5	fxe5
30	Qxg5	e4
31	f6	g6
32	f4	hxg4
33	Be2	gxh3
34	Bh5	Rb2
35	Nh4	Qxf4
36	Qxf4	Bxf4

White resigns

Diagram of final position

Top ratings

The top World Chess Federation ratings for November are Kasparov 2,794pts, Karpov 2,762, Ivanchuk 2,740, Topalov 2,738, Anand 2,735 and Kramnik 2,731. These six will be the participants in Las Palmas. The top ranked British player is Nigel Short on 2692 in world ninth position.

□ Raymond Keene writes on chess Monday to Friday in Sport and in the Weekend section on Saturday.

WINNING MOVE

By Raymond Keene

White to play. This position is from the game Keene — Mestel, Esbjerg 1981. White is threatened with mate in one. What is the best way to deal with this?

Solution on page 50

Figure 27 Newspaper chess column – the highly motivated spend time on it; the unmotivated barely notice it

so-called 'learning curve' is often drawn as a curve, rising first and then levelling off. In reality the graph of learning for many people is nowhere near as smooth. It often consists of rises, falls and the occasional plateau, when learning seems to have stagnated or reached an impasse, and when motivation may have flagged. Hence the importance in the teaching and learning dimension of the curriculum for students to learn to be persistent and to motivate themselves, and for teachers to help them over the flat periods, usually through support and encouragement.

  THINK BOX 7: MOTIVATION

- -

Looking across the third dimension of the cubic curriculum, what examples are there of high and low motivation?

1 Subjects   Are there certain aspects of any subject's content and related activities that appear to reduce motivation? Look at different subjects to see what these might be. Is it especially difficult, or too easy? Is the particular topic remote from the interests and experience of the pupils? Do the pupils need to be more actively engaged in some way?

2 School ethos   What effect does the whole school have on pupils' motivation? Does there appear to be a collective enthusiasm for learning, or is there a dreary downbeat climate? What steps can be taken to create, or enhance further, a positive attitude generally in the school?

3 Individuals   Are there certain pupils who appear to lack motivation? Discuss with some of them what interests, intrigues, confuses, frustrates them. Observe them in lessons to see how they spend their time and the extent to which they are or are not aroused by the tasks they perform in class.

4 Action   In the light of any information gleaned about individuals, what can a teacher or the school in general do to improve motivation? Look at any incentives and rewards that may be on offer, to see whether these appear to have a positive, negative or neutral impact on individuals and groups. Consider forms that are *extrinsic* (given externally, e.g. marks, awards, public commendations) or *intrinsic* (learning to do something for its own sake, deriving personal satisfaction from one's efforts).

Learning styles

A great deal has been written about preferred styles of learning, and there is not space here to cover all these. Suffice it to say that most children, and for that matter most adults, are fairly ignorant about how they learn. Faced with a written examination, many people might intuitively draw up lists, or use a highlighter pen to mark key points they wish to commit to memory, without wondering whether they really do learn best visually. Linguists often have a very good auditory memory, being able to recall clearly the sound of someone's voice, and such people might actually be better off tape recording the key points, rather than trying to use their visual channel exclusively. Few of us have consciously analysed how we best learn, even though we have developed strategies that we might use, or modify, over many decades.

There are many different aspects of learning styles. Some people like to scan a whole page or a scene rapidly, or practise a complete skill, while others prefer to focus on specific parts of it. In field sports, for example, one person may wish to practise the whole of the discus throw, simply repeating the total operation several times, whereas another may work separately on foot movements, the turn across the circle, or the final release of the discus, and then try to put these together. In terms of practice, some people like to distribute their effort over a series of short bursts, while their opposites are happier working more intensively for longer periods at a time. Certain individuals like to work through a subject syllabus in a systematic way, methodically ticking off each topic, exercise or sum when completed, unlike others who prefer to freewheel through the field, exploring and probing.

So far as the curriculum is concerned, this raises interesting issues of principle and practice. Should students only play their strengths, or should they address their weaknesses? In other words, should the 'syllabus-bound' people carry on working through their schedule systematically, ticking off each successful completion as it comes, or should they be encouraged to explore and freewheel, to enhance their repertoire of learning strategies? It ought to be possible for teachers to encourage them to do both – that is, to play to their strengths and exploit their natural strategies, but also to keep an open mind and learn to try other approaches.

Feedback

Knowledge of results, or 'feedback', is a vital ingredient of learning for many people, for without it there are difficulties knowing how one has progressed or what steps to take next. Conventionally feedback is offered in various forms, like written comments or corrections on work that has been marked, or oral discussion. In the case of new interactive technology there is often built-in feedback. The program can be conceived in such a way that correction or comment is an integral part of the process, or that students see immediately the consequence of what they have done. For example, in a science program the student may dismember an atom, or add particles to it, and the screen will demonstrate that a hydrogen atom has now become helium, with the periodic table constantly highlighted on the screen as the student responds, to show what is happening. Alternatively, profiles are assembled showing the student what has been learned or which areas appear strong and which weak. One way or another, knowledge of results offers a valuable tool in the curriculum, and inadequate, confusing or, even worse, inaccurate feedback can mystify and alienate the learner.

TEACHING AND LEARNING

Many of the aspects of learning described here can and should have a considerable impact on the strategies of teaching that might be employed. A matter like the one mentioned above, increasing children's motivation, might involve a variety of moves by the teacher to stimulate curiosity. In this third dimension of the cubic curriculum teachers can use their professional expertise to weave together some of the subject and cross-curricular issues raised in the first and second dimensions.

I am taking 'teaching' here to mean 'whatever teachers do to ensure children learn', as this broad definition goes beyond the important, but narrow concept 'telling', and embraces several strategies in addition to direct instruction. Wang *et al.* (1993) analysed several hundred research studies of the influence of various factors on pupil learning. They concluded that classroom practices exerted a greater effect on what pupils learned than such matters as state and district policies, school demographics or the design and delivery of the curriculum. Within the heading 'classroom practices' it was class management that was most strongly related to pupil learning.

In order to help their pupils learn, teachers will not only have to manage their class effectively, but also give information, ask questions, respond to queries and needs, provide materials and equipment, use whole class, small group and individual teaching, encourage, support, stimulate, intrigue, provoke, delight – a vast repertoire of professional tactics. As has been argued earlier, these very strategies then become themselves an important part of the curriculum, which is why they constitute the third dimension of the cubic curriculum. They are not only the means of communicating information, capitalising on motivation, steering and shaping attitudes, but also models and practices that may influence for many decades to come how people carry on learning, or indeed turn their back on it.

Telling and explaining

Teachers possess knowledge and skills which they are paid to pass on to the next generation. A common strategy for doing this is by telling, passing on information directly rather than circuitously. The act of transmission, however, rarely takes place in dry-cleaned form. Frequently it is accompanied by some sort of amplification, like an explanation, a demonstration, a series of questions and answers to involve the pupils, or some kind of activity to reinforce what is being transmitted through the opportunity for personal practice.

Explaining has often been shown to be the professional skill most esteemed by children themselves (Wragg 1993). Effective explanations incorporate many of the features of learning mentioned above, by being factually accurate, capitalising on curiosity, relating the unfamiliar to the familiar, using an appropriate language register, clearly identifying the essential features of the concept or idea being explained and ensuring that they are understood. Wragg and Brown (1993) analysed teachers' explanations and found a wide range of strategies being employed. Some used approaches similar to those employed by broadcasters, like the 'tease', the intriguing 'In a packed programme tonight we'll be meeting the underwater ballroom dancing champions ...' which is designed to arouse the curiosity of the audience at the beginning of a radio or television programme.

One teacher, introducing the topic 'insects' to a group of 8- and 9-year-olds, began with what Ausubel (1978) called an 'advance organiser', the equivalent of the broadcaster's 'tease', a means of structuring in the mind of the learner the shape of what is to come through an arresting appeal to curiosity:

> If I told you in, say, a bucket of earth there were hundreds of them. They're in the air, they're even in ponds and rivers. There are millions of them in a tree. They live all over the world, except at the North and South Poles. There are over a million different types of them. There are 200,000 different types in this country alone. Some of them can fly, some can swim, some make holes in the ground and some make holes in wood. What do you think I would be talking about?

It was not a superficial attention-gaining gimmick, but rather a successful motivating strategy, rich in information and fascination, designed to maximise the time and arousal that the class would devote to the new topic.

Telling and explaining are important features of teaching, and for children to become lifelong learners they need to be carried out in a well-conceived manner, and also to be factually accurate, so that misconceptions and incorrect information are not committed to memory at an impressionable time. In addition, however, they must provoke further curiosity and generate independence of thought, so that pupils realise they do not know everything they will ever require, but keep a sense of enquiry and have an open rather than a closed mind.

It is a pity that 'telling and explaining' and the next topic, 'discovery and invention', are sometimes seen as being in opposition, for they should be complementary to each other, rather than stark alternatives. Discussion of teaching in the mass media, often provoked by the comment of politicians or ideologues of one kind or another, tends to simplify issues, often by polarising them, as if there are only two mutually antagonistic choices. Hence the constant and stereotyped debate about 'traditional' versus 'progressive' teaching; the use of 'phonics' in the teaching of reading or 'real books'; 'knowledge' versus 'understanding'; 'child-centred' set against 'subject-centred' education.

It is a sterile debate, given that most teachers use a mixture of methods, even if they prefer some approaches to others. Many of the polarisations are simply wrong. It is

Figure 28   Provoking curiosity – explaining a new concept
Source: *Explaining*, Wragg and Brown, Routledge, 1993

perfectly possible for teachers to be interested both in the children and the subjects being taught, rather than only the one at the expense of the other, and putting 'knowledge' and 'understanding' in opposite corners is ludicrous, when both must embrace one another.

Learners need the excitement of finding out, just as they need the confirmation of being told. They also need to engage with the factual as well as with the hypothetical and speculative. It should not be a case of one *versus* the other, but rather a matter of *when* each strategy makes best sense. In adult life we often have to find out for ourselves, but we must also draw on a body of established knowledge and skill that we can summon rapidly and fashion to fit the circumstances.

Take the case of mental arithmetic. Most adults use little mathematics other than elementary number on a daily basis. In the first instance young children may either be told directly, or they may 'discover' that five times four is twenty. They certainly need to *understand* that five fours are the same as four fives, and that both these, just like two tens and ten twos, add up to a total of twenty. Once beyond this first stage of finding out or being told, however, children need to be operational, rather than paralysed by the need either to be told or to have to find out afresh on each occasion.

Giving practice in these 'automatics', therefore, not by chanting them mindlessly in sequence, but by quick response to questions, clustered in conceptual groups, like 'five twos?', 'seven twos?' and so on, is a legitimate way of reinforcing what has either been told or found out, so that it can be used instantly on future occasions. It should not label a teacher as an unreconstructed traditionalist.

Discovery and invention

To discover something is to receive a reward for curiosity, one of the most basic but compelling of human drives. If discovery offers the satisfaction of detecting what is already in existence, then invention is the even greater reward of fashioning something completely novel. From birth onwards most children are so curious about the world around them that they sometimes have to be protected from their own curiosity, for unimpeded exploration of electrical appliances, sharp tools or deep ponds could kill them.

Thrilling though discovery and invention may be, however, they are not only potentially hazardous, but can also be time consuming, frustrating, confusing, inefficient and, at their worst, futile, if nothing results from a quest; hence the need for judicious rather than uncritical use of them, as was mentioned above. None the less, discovery is an important and fundamental form of learning, one from which the learner can draw great satisfaction and a strong sense of ownership. If someone tells us of some magnificently beautiful location and we travel to see it, then this may indeed make an impact on us, but if we stumble on it ourselves, there is a feeling that we own it, even if thousands of others have visited it previously.

The need for humans to discover is paramount, and its place in teaching takes nothing away from other strategies, like 'telling' and 'asking'. Although it is vital to pass on information, in succinct and accurate form, if pupils were only exposed to direct instruction and nothing else then this would be an inadequate preparation for the rest of their lives in the twenty-first century. Much of the time, whether in work or at play, in the absence of a permanent teacher, adults have to be prepared to find out for themselves, using their own initiative to check the quality and accuracy of what they have discovered. They might as well begin preparation for this lifelong assignment during the early stages of their own education.

The opportunities for both discovery and invention are manifold in education, and their place in teaching is not exactly novel. Confucius wrote in his *Analects* 2,500 years ago: 'If out of the four corners of a subject I have dealt thoroughly with one corner and the pupils cannot then find out the other three for themselves, then I do not explain any more.' What Confucius is describing is *guided discovery*, whereby teachers use their own knowledge and experience to set up conditions within which pupils can find out for themselves. I can illustrate this with a personal example.

From time to time I teach a topic like 'magnetism'. I know roughly how magnets work and what they will and will not pick up. If I so wish I can tell this to the pupils in my class. It will not take much time, and there is a fair chance that many will remember what I tell them, if I make it interesting enough. Since I usually teach this topic to relatively young children, aged about 8, I want to make sure they learn about magnets through some kind of personal, meaningful activity.

One strategy available to me is to allow the class to discover for themselves what magnetism is and how it works. The problem is, however, that some students may not even realise that such a phenomenon as magnetism exists. Others may know of it, but not be curious to find out more about it, lacking the necessary prior knowledge, or not having access to appropriate equipment and books. Yet others may be curious, persistent enough to find the time and resources, but not sufficiently knowledgeable to be able to discover the true facts about magnetism, rather than make what might be incorrect suppositions.

Some pupils in a class may of course possess all the prior knowledge, drive, curiosity, imagination and resources to discover the relevant scientific truths for themselves, but this may be a small group, and even these students may develop a few misconceptions along the way, and possibly devote an inordinate amount of time to discovering what is already commonplace knowledge among older people. We could each spend a lifetime randomly discovering the tiniest sliver of what has been learned by previous generations. We might well become very excited, autonomous, lifelong learners, but the human race would slide irrevocably back into ignorance. The art of teaching through discovery lies in capturing the excitement and sense of ownership that comes with finding out for oneself, but not closing down the experience to such an extent that it is lecturing in thin disguise.

My own solution to this dilemma, when teaching about magnetism, is as follows. Each pupil is given 12 objects: a paper clip, a nail, a strip of a tin can, aluminium, copper and brass, a pencil lead, a piece of glass, rubber, plastic, cardboard and wood. These are to be placed into one of two piles, the 'yes' group, which is those objects that magnets are thought to pick up, and the 'no' pile, those believed not to be attracted to magnets. At this point certain misconceptions usually become clear. Many pupils will place all metal objects into their 'yes' group, convinced that magnets attract metals in general, rather than any one particular metal. Some are uncertain where to place the pencil lead, but most are clear that the non-metals, like rubber and plastic, must be put into the 'no' pile.

The next step is for pupils each to be given a magnet and asked to check out their distribution. They soon 'discover' that the magnet will pick up only three of the objects. Many are surprised that brass and copper show no response to the magnet, even more so that aluminium does not, for it is silver and shiny and these are common, if occasionally misleading indicators of magnetic attraction. They find that only the paper clip, nail and strip of tin can are picked up by the magnet. At this point they might easily 'discover' the misconception that magnets pick up objects with tin in them, until I point out that the strip of tin can has iron in it.

The final stage of my own particular way of introducing magnetism is for me to reinforce what has been learned – that magnets pick up things containing iron – through formal reiteration, further discussion and practical work, in which children look for other objects in their environment to which magnets will adhere. What has been learned was acquired through 'discovery', but there were no surprises for the teacher at what was disclosed, for it was 'guided' discovery, finding out within a predetermined structure. I offer this personal example not as a paragon ideal, but simply as an illustration of one way of offering the excitement of discovery and capitalising on curiosity without spending months on futile and possibly misguided exploration.

Although guided discovery may well help pupils to develop and harness their curiosity, it offers only a fairly safe and predictable set of experiences within prescribed circumstances. Guided discovery alone will not necessarily equip them with the independence of mind they need to pursue the elusive and invent the unimagined. For this to be nurtured there must be a proper place for exploration and invention in the curriculum, and several points were made in Chapter 4 about the kinds of thinking necessary for such sideways leaps of the imagination. Since there is usually such a strong place for what is conventional, safe and established in the curriculum, there must also be some room for the unusual, unexpected, unpredicted, even for the eccentric, in the true 'off-centre' sense of that word, even if such activities are sometimes time consuming.

One fruitful teaching strategy lies in the use of different kinds of questions teachers may ask individuals or groups of pupils. The evidence from classroom observation research (Wragg 1993) shows that the vast majority of teachers' questions are either to do with the management of the lesson, or require little extra mental effort beyond the recall of factual information. 'What was the date of the Spanish Armada?' is a perfectly legitimate question on a matter of verifiable historical fact.

What are sometimes called 'higher-order questions', since they demand thinking beyond the level of recall, as described in the previous chapter, are proper questions to ask students to encourage them to use and refine the information they possess. A question like 'Did the United Nations do a good job during the Gulf War?' put to students engaged in the analysis of decision making and influence by international bodies during the twentieth century, will require them to recall facts, synthesise information about various conflicts or disputes and the actions taken by different international agencies such as the League of Nations and the United Nations, and then reach some shrewd evaluation of human conduct. Such questions structure and shape learning, develop critical insight and often engage pupils' interest. Consider the effects, however, of a question like 'What would have happened if the Spanish Armada had won?' This would invite speculation about whether, for example, both Britain and North America might today have been Spanish-speaking Catholic countries. The 'What would happen if . . . ?' type of question is but one of many that can open up a great deal of individual reflection and imagination.

One geography teacher taught a whole lesson around the question 'What would happen if a new motorway were to be built that led directly to our town and beyond?' Not only did it raise matters of fact, like the known effects of motorway building elsewhere, but it also produced intelligent speculation about tourism, trade, communications and the environment. Another teacher asked a class of 9- and 10-year-olds, 'How could a motor car be improved?' There were excited exchanges which produced ideas that were both workable and bizarre. Among suggestions were the use of a continuous jet of air instead of a windscreen, to help cut down accidents from broken glass; putting an engine in each wheel; cars travelling coupled together in convoys and peeling off at the appropriate exit. Questions and other devices that provoke and stimulate the imagination show that unusual ideas and solutions are not solely the preserve of adults or the cleverest pupils, as most children are capable of conceiving novelty.

Group and team work

Sometimes the assumption is made that working in groups is *ipso facto* a good or a bad thing. It was argued earlier that many people have to spend a considerable amount of time·in their adult life as members of a group or team, whether at work, or within their family and community, and that the ability to pool one's knowledge and experience with that of others was an important preparation for the future. Yet teamwork can be as varied in quality as human life itself. There are those team players who are able to enhance both their own and other people's efforts by their membership of a group, and others who can kill a group stone dead from the outset, by lack of co-operation, through denigrating the contributions of others, or by pursuing selfish rather than communitarian ends. Group work in education is not intrinsically good or bad. It varies according to the context, the situation, the membership and the conduct and attitude of the teacher as well as the taught.

Within this third dimension of the cubic curriculum, one important issue is to decide whether group work is in any case the most appropriate method of working. A second is to determine the purpose and nature of the group, which raises questions of selection, who decides on the task, the membership, the programme of work. Third, the conduct of the group needs scrutiny, whether it works harmoniously, what tensions and uncertainties there may be, the extent to which the work is shared or dominated by certain individuals. Although some people become adept at sharing, supporting and the other skills and attributes that are needed in groups, others have to learn to become team members. The effective use of groups has been discussed extensively by Dunne and Bennett (1990).

 THINK BOX 8: TEACHING STRATEGIES

- -

Looking across the teaching strands of the third dimension of the cubic curriculum, consider the following:

1 Telling   Study what happens when teachers tell pupils facts or give direct instruction. Is the factual information accurate? Is it presented in an interesting and engaging way? Is it related to previous learning? What opportunities are there for reinforcement, related activity where appropriate and extension work?

2 Discovering and inventing   Study what possibilities there are for students to find out for themselves and pursue individual or group enquiry. Is there sufficient stimulus to find out? Is there support? Are there problems or misconceptions? Is originality encouraged or discouraged?

3 Teachers' questions   Look at the questions being asked in different subjects and topics. What kind of learning do they appear to foster? Are the questions of one kind or do they stimulate different types of learning? Discuss what has been observed, and draw up a variety of questions that teachers might ask in the circumstances.

4 Feedback   What types of feedback do teachers make available to their students? Look at written comments or corrections, oral discussions and responses to students' answers or suggestions, and the use of any interactive technology or other forms of teaching with built-in feedback.

5 Groups   What use is made of group work during lessons? Are there certain pupils who appear not to participate? If so, why? Study certain groups to see what roles individual pupils play. What is the nature of the group work? Does it involve simply sitting together, or is there genuine collaboration and teamwork?

One major point about the teaching and learning dimension of the cubic curriculum is that, in order to face the exacting world of the future, children need to have experienced a variety of circumstances, challenges to their intellect, teaching strategies, activities, and also that they themselves need to develop an equally wide range of approaches to learning, even if they favour some rather than others. One mode of teaching, one single approach to learning, would be an inadequate basis for the many decades ahead when, as adults, they will have to learn alone or in groups, formally as well as informally, be told as well as find out for themselves, when they are unmotivated or highly motivated.

Teaching and learning strategies need to respond to the *context* in which they take place, a context provided by the first two dimensions. What is appropriate for one subject, topic or activity may not be right for another. That is why it is not desirable to make blanket judgements about such matters as the use of whole-class teaching, individual or group work. Decisions about how pupils should learn and how teachers should teach need to reflect both purpose and context. It would be unfair to expect children to become lifelong enthusiasts for literature, science or history, if they had not been given a basic grounding in the fields, had the opportunity to read about them, pursue relevant activities, ask questions, make inferences, work alone and with others. The decisions about what history book children might read on their own, what class activity they might undertake in science, what group or team project might help develop good citizenship, must all be reached in the light of individual circumstances, not on the basis of some single ideology.

When teachers are telling a story to a class of 5-year-olds, it usually makes best sense to read the story to the whole class, rather than individually to each of 30 or more children. By contrast, if 30 people aged from 17 to 70 want to learn to drive, then they will expect individual practice in actually driving a car, not a mass lecture on the function of the clutch. Anyone wanting to sing in a quartet will need three like-minded people. Matching what is desirable to what is feasible is part of the art of teaching effectively.

CHAPTER SIX

The Whole Model in Action

The curriculum is like an endlessly changing, infinitely variable kaleidoscope. Even if the detail of its content has been determined by an agency or body external to the school or college, there are still thousands of ways in which it can be taught, learned, modulated and extended. Depending on what is the particular focus or concern, the cubic curriculum model put forward in this book can be used in a variety of ways to examine, to invent or to provoke debate about what is happening in the classroom. Its purpose is not to determine the curriculum, for the detail of that must be worked out by those responsible for any individual or group of schools, but rather to enable people to reflect when planning, or to evaluate what is being done.

All three of its dimensions can be considered in a variety of contexts, even when the principal focus is on one of them in particular. If one prime intention behind education is to prepare children for a long and rewarding future, then to ignore either the content of the subjects being taught, the effect of what is being learned on the learner's general development, or the long-term impact of the approaches to teaching and learning being adopted, would be selling them short. It would be like trying to make sausages with a sausage machine and some skins, but no meat.

USING 'SENSOR' CELLS

The following analogy may not be a perfect one, but when trying to check whether something is functioning properly it is common to apply some kind of sensor. For example, a dipstick may be inserted into a tank to check the level of the liquid, a series of thermometers may be used to give temperature readings in different parts of an environment, or various kinds of sensor may be used to feed back information about pressure, chemical change or humidity. What is learned can then be employed to diagnose faults, fine-tune performance, predict future developments or prevent problems. Individual cells and small blocks of cells in the cubic curriculum can be used in a similar manner. Often they relate to specific types of teaching in particular settings, like the way a teacher explains a concept in a geography lesson, or the kind of activities children carry out in science or technology classes.

Consider the following extract from an English lesson, observed during a research project (Wragg 1993), in which the teacher was trying to extend her pupils' vocabulary by discussing certain words that they might use in a story they were to write about a visit to an imaginary island. She began by asking them to imagine what it must be like to visit this island. What we are seeing at this point is activity in *English* in the first dimension, *language* and *thought* in the second dimension, and *discover* and *ask* in the third dimension. Key blocks of cells in the cube are areas like the *English-thought-discover* and the *English-language-ask* cells. After a time she moves on specifically to explore particular words, some of which she elicits from pupils, some of which she gives them or steers them towards. The exchange below occurs in the *English-language-ask* and the *English-language-tell* cells.

Teacher: What would be a good word to describe Darkling Forest?
Pupil: Spooky and creepy.
Teacher: Better than 'spooky and creepy'?
Pupil: Strange and weird.
Teacher: Yes, strange and weird. How about a word beginning with two e's? Do you know it?
Pupil: Eerie.
Teacher: Yes. What does 'eerie' mean?
Pupil: Scary.

Take as another example the ability to perform at a high level as a scientist. Nobel Prize-winning scientists need to have considerable knowledge of their field, but they also need tenacity and determination, a degree of imagination to enable them to go where others have failed to penetrate, as well as the courage to pursue lines of enquiry and action that might fall frustratingly short of their target on many occasions before success is eventually achieved. In terms of schooling, there are particular sensor cells in the cubic curriculum that should help equip someone, not just a future Nobel laureate, with the knowledge, skills and personal qualities that will be required for future achievements. Certainly, any cell which includes science will be of interest, as will those that involve the stimulation of the imagination. Since many successful scientists are leading figures among a group of fellow workers, possibly the chief inspiration of their co-workers, the 'team' channel could be significant.

One key area should be the *science-imagination-discover* cell, so this could be an important sensor when looking at the opportunities available to students in the classroom. Are they given the opportunity to propose, analyse, debate and then test out their own approaches to scientific questions, as well as learn about the tried and tested ways of others? Do teachers ask questions and set up activities that invite intelligent speculation about science, as well as teach the rudiments of it? Is the unusual, the offbeat, the eccentric idea welcomed, regarded with suspicion, or ridiculed? These are just some of the questions that can be asked when looking at classroom life to see what happens in the *science-imagination-discover* cell.

Untrammelled imagination, however, would be useless without the rigour of careful analysis and reflection on the processes and concepts involved. Consider, therefore, another sensor cell, *science-thought-ask*. Do teachers develop their pupils' ability to think critically in science? One teacher was observed telling his class about the characteristics of insects. After a while he switched into question-and-answer mode and the following exchanges took place.

Teacher:	A camel is not an insect. Why?
Pupil:	It hasn't got antennae.
Teacher:	A snail has got antennae.
Pupil:	Insects have wings.
Teacher:	So do nightingales.
Pupil:	Insects collect pollen.
Teacher:	So do humming birds.

It was a jousting but friendly, if slightly adversarial style of teaching that made pupils reflect on their answers. It began with a 'not' analogy (a camel is not an insect), and moved on to provoke pupils to think carefully about making assertions in a scientific context and to be able to defend their arguments. The origins of this type of challenging interaction lie deep in the past, for it was an approach that was not uncommon in Classical Greece, when great debaters, like Protagoras, were able to charge wealthy Athenians 10,000 drachmas to teach their sons public oratory. The name of Socrates became associated with the interrogative form of this strategy when he stated, 'one person who is more knowledgeable than another can, by asking him a series of questions, stimulate the other to think, and so cause him to learn for himself'.

Consider another aspiration in a different field. One of the intentions often expressed by teachers of foreign languages is that their students should learn to express themselves confidently, fluently and accurately in the target language. Suppose someone seeking to achieve this, or wishing to help a teacher with this sort of objective, wanted to identify 'sensor' cells in the cubic curriculum, which might these be? Clearly, the 'modern languages' channel in the first dimension of the cube and the 'language' channel in the second dimension would offer possibilities, but two cells in particular might be worth investigating, namely *modern languages-language-imitate* and *modern languages-language-practise*. Aspects to be studied would include the extent to which the foreign language was being used in the classroom by the students; what kind of talk was in the native and what in the foreign language; the nature of language models on offer to students and the degree of accuracy with which they imitated them; the quality of interaction in the foreign language when native speakers or the teacher were not the model (for example, whether pupils copied one another's errors in pronunciation and intonation, or whether they repeated one another's grammatical and syntactical mistakes).

NATIONAL ASPIRATIONS

Global or national aspirations are often more vague and diffuse than local hopes and intentions. The bigger the scale, the less precise are the aims. A summit conference of national leaders may only be able to agree to reduce international tension or cut down on pollution in the most general terms, whereas an individual teacher may have very specific classroom aspirations, like (for example) seeking to improve the reading performance of a particular child aged 7 by giving more practice in the reading of words which contain the letter combinations '-ight', like 'sight', 'light' or 'night'. She may seek to reinforce a class's ability to understand the nature of fractions in mathematics through the use of three-dimensional models. Meanwhile, the educational aims of the government of her country may be much less well defined, perhaps aspiring to 'improve national literacy levels', or 'raise performance in mathematics'.

Korea is an interesting example of publicly stated aspirations for the twenty-first century. It is a country that moved rapidly from a principally agrarian society to having a $166 billion volume of trade by 1993. The aims of Korean education for a prosperous future are stated in official documents to be 'humanisation, refinement, informativeness, human welfare and open-mindedness', and the intention is to raise 'a self-reliant individual equipped with a distinct sense of independence, a creative individual with a sense of originality, and an ethical individual with sound morality and democratic citizenship'.

In order to translate these often well-intended, but diffuse notions into action, a government must harness the support and co-operation of teachers, for no country's ruling body can raise pupils' achievements or develop their character from a distance. National aspirations do not take immediate effect in thousands of classrooms by osmosis. Let us take as an example the wish that the Korean education system must foster more 'individualism'. The concept may need a sharper definition. There is a belief that children should learn to be more self-reliant, that they should be capable of greater imagination and independence. Is there also a hope that more individuals will learn to solve problems or invent novelties? Or a fear that there will be greater egoism, more self-centred behaviour and beliefs, since there is also a mention of ethics, morality and democratic citizenship? In any case, notions of 'citizenship' can vary, and the report by the Speaker's Commission (1990) on citizenship in the United Kingdom was undertaken against a different set of cultural assumptions from that in Korea.

National aspirations may require changes to take place in each of the dimensions of the cubic curriculum, starting with the subject content, particularly if there is a desire to improve citizens' knowledge of a whole field, like 'technology' or 'history'. The wish for more 'individualism', however, is perhaps better addressed across the other two dimensions of the cube. The cross-curricular 'language', 'thought' and 'imaginative' channels of the second dimension are worth special scrutiny. Indeed, it would be perfectly possible to insert a channel in the second dimension of the cubic curriculum model and simply call it 'individualism'.

In terms of the third dimension of the cube, teaching and learning, if the predominant or even sole form of instruction is didactic, with pupils required to copy, listen and respond only to given commands, then in order to create greater autonomy, it may be necessary to foster a shift away from the channels 'tell' and 'imitate', so there can be a move more towards 'discover' and 'ask'. Independence of mind is not usually achieved solely through obeying the commands of one's superiors, with no opportunity to practise autonomous decision making.

There would be many sensor cells that could be explored to see if greater individualism were being fostered in schools and colleges. These include such cells as *history-thought-discover* or *art-imagination-practise*, depending on the particular focus being adopted. Observation and analysis of classroom processes in different subject and thematic areas should reveal the extent to which individualism is being fostered. The issue, however, like many similar matters, is wider than just the subject content of lessons on the timetable. What happens in the whole school, both inside and outside the classroom, is of interest. Scrutiny of the school's ethos, its beliefs and practices is also necessary, for these are a legitimate part of what is sometimes called the 'hidden curriculum'. The extent to which students are given responsibility in the school, their involvement in choices about their own programme, the degree of respect accorded to them, all these are portions of messages which, subtly or crudely, course through and around their day-to-day lives.

Some national and ethnic beliefs and aspirations are concerned with the social

Figure 29   Art lesson and 'individualism'

climate in which learning takes place. Many Afro-Americans support the African communitarian ideal of 'connecting', the notion that people belong to a large family which helps and supports its members, a belief which is shared by other groups. It is perfectly possible to use the cubic curriculum model to investigate the extent to which this is a reality in a school. Again the focus goes beyond the classroom and will be particularly marked along the 'social/citizenship' and 'team' channels. In this context scrutiny of the 'team' channel might concentrate not just on nurturing ability to be a member of some collaborative group, but the extent to which teachers support their pupils and the degree and nature of support that the pupils offer one another. Deliberately checking that support actually exists, in a practical and regular form, offers a means of ensuring that notions of 'community' and 'family' are a reality and not mere rhetoric.

There are many caveats to consider over these various national and global aspirations. The first is their very diffuse nature. Unless there is clarification of often well-intended, but potentially empty or highly ambiguous concepts such as 'individualism', 'community', 'citizenship' or 'whole person', then it is difficult for teachers to secure them, students to aspire to them, or, more fundamentally, for anyone to check whether they are being realised at all. Second, there needs to be some consideration of the extent to which governments or international movements can and should influence directly what happens in classrooms. Different nations and faiths have different expectations. In some cultures it is regarded as perfectly proper for the state or the ruling body to determine the nature of classroom subjects and processes. In others, state or external intervention is anathema.

There is another very important related matter, which is that some national aspirations require a major shift in attitude and practice if they are to be successfully implemented. It is all too easy to have a national desire which is not matched by a national effort of any weight. The desire for greater 'individualism', for example, cannot succeed unless there is a climate that tolerates and encourages people to act as individuals. Otherwise it would be like equipping new surgeons with all the skills of transplant surgery, only to find that the hospitals in which they worked still believed in the use of leeches. This particular aspiration is an interesting one. If it succeeds and people really do leave school able to operate autonomously, then there can be considerable threats to the *status quo*, even to social cohesion, unless their hard won autonomy is applied to the greater good in a positive and constructive way.

People encouraged to be individuals can sometimes be uncomfortable to live with, mavericks who challenge orthodoxy and regularly posit alternatives to existing practice that may threaten those who represent or cherish what is currently done. For some this uncertainty would offer an exciting prospect, for others a worrying one, threatening to replace orderliness with anarchy. But when ordinary people first received free public education, there were those who argued against universal literacy on the grounds that it might encourage the masses to revolt.

The successful adoption of a national or large-scale aspiration can only come about if the teachers who have to secure it are able to change what they do in their classrooms, and this requires a change to the deep structures of their daily practice, a matter that is discussed further below. There is a limit to what a government or ruling body can do to bring this about, especially in a democratic society. The evidence from my own studies of teacher behaviour after being appraised (Wragg *et al.* 1996) shows that change is more likely to come about when teachers are committed to securing it and believe that they are party to it, rather than when they resent the imposition of something for, as they would see it, no good reason. National initiatives, therefore, are best achieved if teachers feel involved in what is happening, if support is provided, and if there is some monitoring of change and its effects. An example of ways in which the development of 'individualism' might be monitored is shown in Think Box 9.

 THINK BOX 9: IS 'INDIVIDUALISM' BEING DEVELOPED?

- -

1 **Defining**   What is meant by 'individualism'? What sort of personal knowledge, skills, attitudes and behaviour would be needed to bring it about?

2 **Sensor cells**   Which cells in the cubic curriculum are likely to be most fruitful in helping pupils attain the kind of autonomy envisaged? Which aspects of teaching and learning would it be most worth while to study? What cells might be investigated to study the extent to which individualism is harmonious and constructive, rather than destructive and anarchic?

3 **Activities and tasks**   Look at the activities being undertaken in different subjects and topics. What kind of pupil response do they produce? Are the activities of the kind that will encourage members of the class to think and act for themselves, or are pupils too dependent on others? Consider also the pupils' experiences within the school, but outside the classroom. Discuss what is observed and see what might be needed to encourage greater pupil independence.

4 **Teachers' responses**   What is the response of teachers when children act in an independent way? Is such behaviour tolerated? encouraged? discouraged? What sources of information are available to the class? Are they solely dependent on the teacher's knowledge, or are there other forms of reference on hand? If so, what use is made of them by the pupils? If not, what might be provided?

NEW TECHNOLOGY AND THE 'SOCIAL' DIMENSION

At the beginning of this book it was argued that the creation of more jobs in service and support, leisure and recreation, rather than in factories, meant that *social skills*, the ability to get on with others, might in future become more valued. The increasing use of new interactive technology, whereby children are encouraged to sit before a screen, or don a helmet and enter a 'virtual reality' environment, learning from huge databases in the process, may at first seem inimical to social development. After all, it can easily become a private matter.

The learner may enter a world which appears not to involve fellow human beings directly, since 'conversations' about subject matter, and 'answers' to queries are provided through the interactive facilities of the machine's software, by surrogate and illusory, rather than by real people. Yet it is perfectly possible to use interactive media in a way that will enhance rather than extinguish social competence. There is, of course, nothing wrong with a student being immersed in the study of, say, the history of the Second World War, through a television screen and keyboard. Indeed, depending on the quality of text, graphics, film, sound and animation available, some pupils might learn a great deal more than they would from print alone. As a form of private study it is not all that different from being absorbed in a good book. When pupils read a book alone there is usually rejoicing from the adults around them, rather than anxiety that they may turn into unrepentant hermits.

One way to elicit whether interactive technology is offering opportunities for, rather than replacing social interaction, is to look at classroom processes along the 'social/citizenship' and 'team' channels of the second and third dimensions of the cubic curriculum. One useful sensor might be the *history-social-team* cell, which should reveal, for example, whether pupils discuss what they are learning with others in their group, or whether their studies are undertaken in isolation. Working alone to find out information, and later sharing or interpreting it with others, is a valuable part of social development. Activities in this part of the curriculum can also usefully stress the need for children to check that information is accurate, before passing it on to others as authoritative, another valuable insight into how to play a useful and reliable social role.

There are many other possibilities for looking at social development, or the lack of it. One can study the extent to which pairs or small groups working collaboratively at an actual work station share the activities, help each other with searching, recording, analysing, formulating new questions to pursue, deciding which medium or database to utilise, all these can make positive contributions to the growth of social competence. Interactive media do not have to be used in cold solitude.

LIFELONG EDUCATION AND LEARNING THROUGH SUCCESS

Will children be so enthused in school that they are encouraged to continue learning throughout what it is to be hoped will be very long lives? The answer to this, one of the most telling questions that can be asked in education, may be sought within each of the three dimensions of the cubic curriculum. If students have not learned the operational and organising subject matter and skills they need, then there would be nothing on which to build. Should the development of their language, thought and personal qualities have been neglected, then they would have neither the competence nor the tools for lifelong learning. If they have been badly taught, their curiosity has been stifled, and they have concluded that learning itself is dreary rather than exciting and fulfilling, then they will have no appetite for further study. They will see learning not as an immense boon to the human race, a lifelong passport to interesting and rewarding experiences, but rather as something at which they have failed ignominiously. At its grudging best, education will be seen as a necessary expedient to obtaining a better-paid job; at worst, as a self-inflicted torture.

There are many questions that can be addressed. The example of number work within mathematics is an interesting case in point. One question that is often asked is why children in Germany or Taiwan appear to perform better in mathematics than British children. The gap appears to be larger in the particular field of *number*, rather than *geometry* or *probability*. I have frequently visited Germany to observe lessons in German schools, asking myself whether there might be classroom evidence worth considering. This is very much informal observation, rather than research-based study, as it is difficult to assemble a list of 'comparable' schools, classrooms and teachers in different countries, and I am usually in schools for purposes other than formal classroom research.

The explanation for such differences as may exist could lie outside the classroom and be rooted in the cultural traditions of that state concerned, in that schooling in general and mathematics in particular may be taken more seriously by German children and their families, or by the community, or that children in one country have more opportunities outside school to use number than those in another country. There may, however, be factors at work inside the classroom, albeit under the influence of forces from outside it.

Most of the mathematics we use in adult life is to do with number and measures, rather than geometry or algebra, as was said earlier. If children leaving school are not fluent in their handling of numbers, then this can blight lifelong learning, as well as inhibit them in both domestic and working life. Numeracy is an important 'meta-language' (that is, a language about language), which can pervade, for good or ill, many transactions in child and adult life.

All of which raises further important questions. In their mathematics lessons, should children learn only about number, on the grounds that this is the most frequent area of use in adult life? Surely not, as this would be a narrow and dreary view of the subject. In any case, even if one takes a purely instrumental view of mathematics, other aspects of it do figure in adult daily life, such as *shape* (will six-sided floor tiles fit together?), *measures* (how many litres of fuel shall we need for this journey?), *handling data* (how do the sunshine charts for Florida compare with those of New York?), and *space* (which is the shortest route between two towns?). Algebra too may be useful when finding the unknown (if my final bill includes $17\frac{1}{2}$

per cent tax, then how much was the original charge without tax?).

If one rejects the temptation, therefore, to resort to what would probably be a self-defeating concentration on oversimplified basics, the question still remains: if German children are indeed better at handling number than are British children, why is this the case? Part of the answer may lie in the sensor cell *mathematics (number)-thought-practise*. One major weakness, particularly among British children of average and below-average ability, is in the particular kind of rapid thought required to handle what are known as 'multiplication facts'. In real life adults often have to make quick responses to questions about multiplication. The most common algorithm which adults would use when buying five items at 70 pence each involves a rapid recall of '$5 \times 7 = 35$' and then adding a zero to make the adjustment for place value. Some might use addition and simply add five 70s together, and some might even need pencil and paper, but those who are instantaneously numerate would respond almost automatically.

In the German primary classes I have observed, there has been a greater occurrence of rapid practice of instant responses to multiplication questions than in comparable British primary classes. This is not the same as mindless chanting of tables, nor were rapid oral exchanges the sole means of practising. Furthermore, most pupils seemed to understand what it was they were doing, so it was not mere mechanical imitation. In German secondary schools too there was more oral practice for those who still needed it, and the following exchange was recorded in a Hauptschule in a class of 12-year-olds of average and below-average ability:

Teacher:	Right, are you ready? Quick, quick! Seven eights?
Pupil 1:	Fifty-six.
Teacher:	Yes. Five sevens?
Pupil 2:	Thirty-six.
Teacher:	Oh, Karl, think about it.
Pupil 2:	No. Thirty-five.
Teacher:	Yes, good. Next time. Nine threes?
Pupil 3:	Twenty-seven.
Teacher:	Wonderful, Dieter. Karl, are you ready? Five sevens?
Pupil 2:	Thirty-five.
Teacher:	Five sevens are thirty-five, excellent, Karl.

This exchange is not being put forward as an argument for endless drill. I have seen similar transactions in British schools, but I have witnessed more in German classrooms. It represents some of the ingredients thought to be associated with achievement, particularly *time spent on the task with some degree of success* (Denham and Lieberman, 1980), *arousal* and *positive expectations*. The interaction reported above was conducted amid good humour, and Karl's 'second chance' followed almost immediately after his first failure. The teacher's expectation that he would succeed next time was clearly signalled. Many adults terminate their education when they leave school because they believe they were failures at learning. School can easily become a place where people actually learn how to fail through repeated experience of not being successful. Constant unredeemed failure is not proper bedrock for lifelong learning, whereas supported and reinforced success is, so it is worth looking at classroom life to see how much of it conditions failure and how much sets up success.

'OPPORTUNITY TO LEARN' AND CLASSROOM MANAGEMENT

Closely related to the notion of success is the whole question of opportunity. Unless pupils actually have the chance to learn something in the first place, they are not likely to acquire relevant knowledge through the ether. When I carried out a study of teachers' explanations to children (Wragg 1993), one of the experiments we did was to set up experimental and control groups to see whether giving children the opportunity to learn made any difference to their performance. Matched groups were given tasks to perform, including writing an imaginative essay and learning scientific concepts. The experimental groups had short lessons on the topic with their teacher before completing the test papers, which their teachers had not seen, while the control groups simply had to complete the tasks without any preparation. The markers did not know whether the papers they marked had been completed by members of the experimental or control groups.

The results showed no differences between groups on some measures, but the creative writing of the experimental groups was scored significantly higher on 'imaginativeness', 'coherence' and 'length', and their factual knowledge about scientific concepts was also significantly greater. However, it was particularly interesting when we analysed the lessons given to the experimental groups to see what features of 'insects' teachers mentioned. They had been told that children would be asked to look at a variety of creatures afterwards and say whether or not they were insects. Highest scores on the test were obtained in classes where teachers were more likely to mention characteristics of insects, such as 'feelers', 'abdomen' and 'thorax'. Those classes that had not been given the opportunity to learn these concepts simply did less well on the identification test.

There are several ways in which different aspects of 'opportunity' can be studied using the cubic curriculum model. They relate to important issues about school and classroom management. Indeed, 'management' as a thematic label might easily be included in the third dimension of the cubic curriculum, for it was identified in the large-scale summary of research by Wang *et al.* (1993), cited in the previous chapter, as a critical influence on learning. It was not possible to include all the teaching and learning categories I should have liked in the foreshortened model of the cubic curriculum shown in the diagrams in this book, but that does not mean that it is not an important channel. In my own studies of teachers' class management in primary and secondary schools (Wragg 1984 and 1993) I have analysed hundreds of lesson observations, and many of the strategies that teachers use when managing learning, time and space, behaviour or resources involve transactions that would lie in the 'personal' 'social', 'tell' and 'ask' channels of the second and third dimensions, like reprimanding, or asking for explanations.

Various school management issues occur in the first dimension of the cube, where the standing of the subject can be studied. How much time is allocated to it? If the subject or topic were not there on the timetable at all, then there would be no official opportunity to learn it. The second dimension is also relevant, as the subject or field may emerge 'officially' in the first dimension, but more informally in the second. The example of 'numeracy' is again of interest here. It may be firmly located in the subject of mathematics on the public timetable, but teachers' individual management of their own and their pupils' time will determine whether there are also opportunities to acquire numeracy in other subjects, like science, technology, history, geography, or in a cross-curricular theme such as 'health education', where pupils might collect data on themselves and their lifestyles, as well as analyse and display their results.

Another aspect of the second dimension that can be investigated is the extent to which fair opportunities are available to all, and not just to a few pupils, another classroom management issue, this time in terms of pupil behaviour and the extent to which they are given access to information, resources, books, equipment, teachers' time and attention. All these are an important part of children's education, both in terms of the subjects and topics they are studying and the hidden curriculum transmitted though the messages they pick up about their own worth or their place in society.

If some children manage to gain considerable access to resources while others do not, or if some pupils are allowed to disrupt the education of their fellows, then the opportunity to learn is not being distributed on a fair basis. For example, it has sometimes been noted that boys rush over to computers or technical equipment ahead of girls; that when three pupils carry out a science experiment or an assignment, two of them may collude to exclude the third; that children who are reticent may have less chance to answer teachers' questions or take part in oral exchanges and practice than those who thrust themselves forward; that leadership roles are often taken on by the same pupils, even if there are others perfectly capable of performing the necessary functions.

The biggest killer of all is low expectations, one of the most common and potent criticisms of teaching. Those of whom too little is expected, and this can include children of all abilities, may find their aspirations and achievements limited or grounded, as they are unwittingly denied a fair opportunity to reach their potential. This is a good example of the need to use the model intelligently. A model such as this cannot possibly, of itself, identify low expectations, any more than a microscope could make important discoveries without human intelligence. But sensitive scrutiny of the activities highlighted when using the model may pick up something.

Add in the third dimension and opportunities to learn something like 'numeracy' can be considered in much more precise form, as several possible blocks of sensor cells can be investigated, such as *science-language/thought-practise* or *geography-numeracy-tell*. If numeracy really is being developed, then some of the opportunities to increase competence in it should reveal themselves through analysis of the various appropriate activities, explanations, exercises, conversations that are observed during

THINK BOX 10: OPPORTUNITY TO LEARN – NUMERACY

1 Where to look   Which elements in the cubic curriculum are likely to be most fruitful in helping pupils secure the opportunity to learn to be more numerate? Which subjects or cross-curricular themes (a) already offer possibilities, and (b) might afford scope for practice? What aspects of teaching and learning would it be most worth while to study?

2 Activities and tasks   With a specific focus on what the pupils actually do, look at the activities being undertaken in different subjects and topics that will arguably enhance children's numeracy. What kind of response do they produce? Do the activities offer further practice of existing knowledge and skill? new learning? What might be the balance between practice of old and fresh learning?

3 Coherence   Are the opportunities to improve numeracy scattered or grouped in some way? Look across several subjects or activities and see if numeracy appears to be covered in a coherent way, or whether it is contradictory and confusing. Discuss what is observed with the teacher(s) concerned, and see what might be necessary to enhance what their pupils achieve. Are the knowledge and skills acquired in one context transferable to another?

4 Strategies of teaching and learning   What is the nature of interactions between teachers and pupils during numeracy-related activities or exchanges? Does it seem likely that what is taking place will enhance numeracy? Is there any evidence that learning is taking place and that knowledge and skill are being improved? Do pupils seem to have a positive or negative attitude to their work in this field? Is there anything the teacher might do to improve opportunities to learn and increase children's chances of success?

5 Fair opportunities   Are there some children who seem to have fewer or no opportunities, compared with their fellows? If so, who are they? In what way and for what reason do they seem to have less opportunity to learn? Are expectations too low? What can be done to improve their chances? Does teachers' classroom management enhance or impede opportunities?

lessons. If few such events are noted, then teachers trying to sponsor improved numeracy should review what they and their pupils do, so as to increase opportunities for worthwhile activities. Both quality and quantity of opportunity are important.

CITIZENS OF THE FUTURE

The dangers of an uneducated citizenry being exploited by some of the predators in any society were mentioned at the beginning of this book. People will need to know their rights and entitlements, as well as their obligations to others, if they are to play a full part in society and not be exploited by the unscrupulous. In Chapter 4 there was a discussion of the place of citizenship in the second dimension of the model. The curriculum may not be the sole influence on children and adults during their education, but it is none the less a powerful vehicle for shaping the future. It equips the next generation to determine their own and other generations' future by arming them with the means by which they can influence events, rather than be the eternal victims of them. In times gone by, millions died of diseases that are nowadays routinely curable. It was the curriculum in schools, colleges and universities that gave the tools of innovative enquiry, experiment and practice to those medical experts who developed new treatments and cures.

It is difficult to decide how well children are being prepared for the rest of their lives when the future itself is so uncertain. At the beginning of this book a number of hypotheses were put forward about possible factors that could affect society in the twenty-first century, when more time may be spent away from the workplace and in the home or community. There may also be less personal physical activity and more spectating; changes in the Four Ages will require continued learning and the flexibility to adapt as people switch jobs and enjoy a longer period of healthy retirement; the ability to get on well with one's fellows will become a more important personal and social quality, as teamwork becomes a common requirement; wide rather than rudimentary knowledge, a broad range of skills and traits, and the ability to learn from others and find out for oneself, often using interactive technology, will be essential prerequisites for lifelong autonomy; as knowledge expands, fields of expertise may continue to narrow.

There are several ways in which the cubic model can be used to see how the curriculum appears to be preparing people for life in the future, and many of these have already been described. These different applications are the basis of a broad view of education, and they are relevant to life inside and outside the classroom and the formal structure of the timetabled curriculum. They include the ones below.

Whole curriculum

The overarching question that needs to be asked is whether the curriculum, in all its dimensions, provides the balance of knowledge, skills, experiences that will offer a strong base for further development. Is there both the breadth to give students a firm foundation for what they will need, as well as the depth, where necessary, to avoid mere superficial coverage of too wide a field? Are there gaps and omissions that should be repaired?

Individual dimensions

Each of the dimensions can be used separately to see the extent to which students are being equipped with suitable knowledge, skills and experiences (1) within each of the scheduled subjects, (2) coherently across the curriculum, and (3) through the various means of teaching and learning being employed. Examples cited above include analysing the content of a science course, the development of language ability in different subjects, and the extent to which students are exposed to different methods of teaching.

Individual cells

Any cell of the cubic curriculum may reveal insights into more specific questions, often related to well-defined purposes, like the opportunity to learn something through various means and media. Examples given earlier include the extent to which children are able to practise automatic responses to mental calculations, or whether aesthetic or moral aspects of technology and science are explored.

It is worth repeating, however, that *the cubic curriculum is not meant to be used in a narrow, philistine or prescriptive way.* There is more to designing and implementing a curriculum than merely limiting it to what our frail judgement may decree at one particular moment in time. Although education needs, and to some extent is, a vision of the future, a purely instrumental curriculum, where everything has to have an explicit and identifiable purpose, would be dreary and restrictive.

Equally, it would be self-defeating to propound a model of the curriculum which was supposed to help prepare young people to be both sociable team members and autonomous individuals, yet which was entirely operated and determined by their teachers. If people really are to play a significant role as significant stakeholders in the exciting but challenging world of the twenty-first century, who will drive their own affairs, instead of being entirely dependent on others for everything, then they should be encouraged to participate in decisions during their education. Autonomy must be rehearsed and earned, rather than something that comes with the birthday presents at the age of majority. The participation of future citizens in the evaluation and determination of their own education is something to which I shall return towards the end of this chapter.

MAKING YOUR OWN CUBE

The cubic model is a flexible one. The version described above is principally one that is suitable for schools trying to cover a widely based curriculum with children of compulsory school age. It can easily be adapted, however, to suit a variety of situations. The main dimensions can be modified, as can the labels attached to each channel. What is important is first of all that the curriculum concerned should not be seen in its narrowest form, as a list of contents and nothing else, and second that the model should be used to gain insight into what is actually being achieved, so that whatever steps are necessary can be taken to improve the nature and quality of what students learn.

The model can be a broad or a narrow one, and these terms are not meant to be pejorative. A broad version of a vocational curriculum aimed at students on a general pre-vocational course, for example, might look like the one in Figure 30.

An even more focused cubic curriculum in a more tightly defined field, such as a programme of research training for a higher degree, might have fewer cells as the scope is narrower, but the model again does not of itself tell one anything about the depth or appropriateness of the curriculum. That is for intelligent users of the model to surmise.

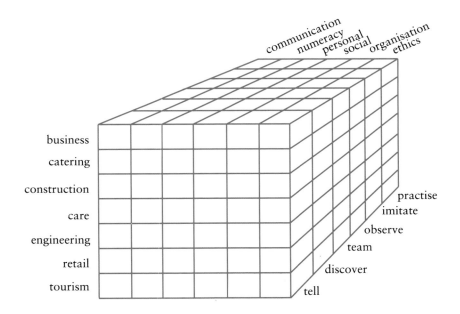

Figure 30   Broad vocational model of the cube

There are many other ways in which bespoke, purpose-built cubic models can be conceived. These might incorporate different dimensions, such as the emotions, for example. It is also theoretically possible to stand a cube on its side and make the first dimension cross-curricular issues, or teaching and learning strategies. It is difficult to conceive of a credible curriculum, where process would take priority over substance, but it could be done.

HOW DO SCHOOLS AND TEACHERS CHANGE?

At the beginning of this book I described the rapidly changing world which will be inhabited by today's pupils in the coming years. Just as society is reshaping and altering, in some cases on a daily basis, so too must schools and colleges modify and adapt, sometimes following or mirroring what happens in the outside world, sometimes ignoring it, as short-lived fashions come and go, but well-established values and patterns survive. Indeed, schools and colleges can afford to be even more ambitious, for they can make a highly significant contribution to determining and shaping the future. Pupils in school today will play an important role in their various jobs, families and communities within a decade of leaving, and may become highly influential on them in the two or three decades after that. Properly educated they can shape for the good the destiny of their nation and indeed that of the whole planet for a significant part of the twenty-first century. If they are badly educated, however, then society would slide irrevocably back into primitive squalor.

Schools that change – dynamic practitioners

In order to avoid such a relapse, schools themselves must change what they do, so that their pupils are well fitted to become citizens of this rapidly changing world. But they must change judiciously, not merely follow fashion uncritically. This requires what I have called elsewhere (Wragg 1994) *dynamic practitioners in dynamic schools*, that is, teachers who can reflect on and then change what they do for the better, thereby creating a school which adapts and improves itself as a matter of course. The multi-dimensional model I have described in this book is but one device that can help teachers address what they are trying to achieve through this wider view of the curriculum. It tries to depict the curriculum as much more than a mere collection of subjects and syllabuses, but rather as a set of intricately linked dynamic processes, open to intelligent scrutiny and modification.

It is quite difficult for teachers to change in isolation, however. The climate within the school might not encourage change, teachers may be rewarded for following authority, not rocking the boat, playing safe. Yet for children's education to improve, schools and teachers must change, otherwise everything remains the same, and that is only justifiable if a state of perfection has been reached.

There needs to be a collective will to do things better, and this is often a mark of a successful school, that it changes not according to whim, fashion or diktat, but judiciously. If teachers can work together to hone one another's professional skills, to reflect on the curriculum and modify what is done as is necessary, then the school can be said to be 'dynamic', as opposed to 'static'. The cubic curriculum model may help not only with looking at present practice, but possibly stimulate teachers to devise unusual and novel ways of grouping subjects, devising topics and activities, relating their strategies to their aims and intentions. It would be an intriguing prospect if it did even a small amount of that. Team approaches to twenty-first-century problems and challenges, as was stressed at the beginning of this book, can bring exciting results.

Deep and surface structures – teachers who change

Many experienced teachers work hard at improving their own subject knowledge and professional skills, such as explaining, questioning, assessing progress, helping those with learning difficulties, raising pupils' aspirations and achievements, while others fall into a routine of settling for their existing subject knowledge and setting tasks which may be unexacting for many of their pupils. An important study by Bennett *et al.* (1984), cited earlier, offered an interesting insight into some of the questions raised when using the cubic curriculum model. They analysed the tasks that children were set and the extent to which these matched their ability and the current state of their knowledge and skill.

Dynamic practitioners review and reflect on what their classes are doing. They then modify their curriculum and their own strategies as the need arises. Bennett and his colleagues describe a scene which shows a 7-year-old pupil struggling to achieve literacy. It illustrates beautifully how, in order to improve the quality of pupils' learning, the curriculum must be seen as multi-dimensional:

Alan was given a writing assignment. His teacher showed him a set of cards, each of which illustrated people at work, and suggested that he write about one of them. He selected a card showing a bus driver and took it to his desk. He paused for 5 minutes, apparently thinking about what to write. Eventually the teacher approached and asked him what his first sentence was going to be. He replied, 'I went on a bus to school'. He started his writing and then searched through his word book for 'school'. He failed to find it and consulted his teacher. She helped him spell it and then explained about the 'sleepy c'. He went back to his desk and continued to write for several minutes, reading aloud as he wrote. He hesitated over the word 'sometimes' and went to the teacher to ask how to spell 'times'. There was a queue at the teacher's desk. Whilst waiting he found the word under 't' in his word book and shouted out to the teacher, 'I've found it miss. It's here'. A few minutes later he went to the teacher again to ask how to spell 'gives'. . . . Twenty-three minutes after choosing the workcard Alan took his story out to have it marked. He had written, 'I went to school on the bus and I went home on the bus sometimes the bus driver gives me something to eat Im going homs I am going to sleep til morning.'

If the teacher wished to improve what is happening here, then several aspects of the cubic curriculum are relevant, like the *English-language-discover* cell. Alan is sent away to find out some information and then write about it, a task with which he seems to need more help, not only in terms of his own knowledge and skill in English, but also in his ability to organise himself and act independently.

Each of the dimensions of the cubic model is of interest – the subject (Was the topic appropriate? Does he have the necessary knowledge?); the cross-curricular (Is this improving language, thought, behaviour?); the teaching and learning (How useful is his wordbook? What help would he need to be able to use a simple dictionary? How could the teacher generate more pupil independence, so the queues of word seekers disappear and she is free to help those with real problems, or stimulate to higher and further levels of activity those who finish assignments rapidly?).

One huge problem faced by teachers wishing to change their classroom behaviour is the sheer speed and volume of transactions in many classrooms. Wragg (1994) reports different studies showing that teachers engaged in as many as 1,000 interpersonal exchanges in a single day; that there was a change in 'activity' every five to eighteen seconds, an average each lesson of 174 changes in who talked and who listened; that teachers often made a decision in less than a second. In the circumstances it is astonishing that teachers are able to scan so many factors at all in the short time available – which pupils are concerned, their background and prior history, their ability, behaviour, demeanour, level of maturity and a host of others.

The result of these vast numbers of repeats and rehearsals of favoured strategies is that teachers lay down deep structures which lie beneath their patterns of teaching. If they had to reflect fully on every conceivable one of the millions of interactions in their professional career, they would be paralysed. Above these deeply laid-down structures are more superficial ones that may come and go, and so they lie just beneath the surface of their decisions. Deep structures in particular do not change in a trice. They have taken too long to lay down for that to happen.

The notion of the teacher researcher (Stenhouse 1975) and the reflective practitioner (Schoen 1983) are attractive means whereby teachers can improve the way they teach the curriculum. But in order to be effective, reflection must be related to action. The research literature (Wragg 1994) shows clearly that there is no single good teacher stereotype, so there is no case for saying that all teachers in a school should teach in like manner. The dynamic school is not a place where everyone is the same, each teacher a clone of the others. It is, rather, a place where there is a collective commitment to working collaboratively to improve teaching in the whole school. The model in this book can be used as a means towards contemplating and implementing judicious change, and therefore, it is hoped, improvement, by both individuals and groups.

Pupils who change

This raises again the issue of the role of the pupils in school improvement. It is all very well for teachers to be reflective and dynamic, but there is little point in all this reflection and dynamism if it makes no impact on the students. Today's pupils are tomorrow's citizens, so they are important potential architects of our future well-being. If they are thought to be knowledgeable and insightful about teaching, then they should be much more directly involved in discussions about teaching and learning. Schmuck and Schmuck (1975) describe how the teacher can sensitise children working in groups to the processes involved, and capitalise on their natural insights to make them partners in learning, rather than merely the recipients of teaching.

If pupils are partners in the negotiation of change and improvement, then to some extent they need to be aware of some of the factors that teachers know about, including how they learn. This is sometimes called *metacognition*, knowing about how they think and learn. If they are aware of classroom processes and teaching and learning strategies, then they may be in a position to fulfil the hope expressed earlier that citizens of the twenty-first century will be autonomous, as well as team learners, for many decades to come.

Gage and Berliner (1984) describe what is involved in this kind of self-awareness. They include in their list the ability to make and refine predictions, maintain focus, relate ideas to existing knowledge, ask questions of themselves, pick out important information, dismiss irrelevant information, recognise relationships, use visualisation when reading and problem solving, consider the worth of ideas, and know when to ask for help. There are other characteristics and skills that can be added. The final exercise in Think Box 11 is but one means of involving pupils, depending on their age and maturity, in the analysis and direction of their own learning. The development of both autonomy and the ability to work and live as a member of harmonious groups is not an impossible dream, difficult though it may be to achieve. In the complex changing world of the third millennium these attributes will be essential.

THINK BOX 11: THINKING ABOUT TEACHING AND
LEARNING

- -

1 **Age and maturity**   Consider the age and maturity of the pupils
concerned. Are they very young and so may have relatively little
experience on which to draw, or are they older and more mature?
How far can they be influential on what they learn, and to what
extent can they take part in discussions about their own learning
and their future as citizens?

2 **Reflecting on the future**   Discuss the pupils' own vision of the
future, giving, as appropriate, information about changes and
trends in society. How do they see the future? What do they see as
the principal purposes of education? What views do they have on
the kinds of knowledge, skills and experiences that may help them?
Do they have a particularly restricted view about what is 'useful',
rejecting much of what they are expected to learn as useless?

3 **Activities and tasks**   Encourage pupils to think about the tasks
and activities they are currently undertaking. How are these
supposed to fit in with what they have learned in the past and what
they might learn in the future within the subject or topic? How
might they learn these more effectively? Talk to pupils on their own
or together to see if there are particular problems that individuals
or groups experience.

4 **Using the cube**   This will clearly vary according to the age and
maturity of the class, but without bewildering the members of it
with detail, try to discuss some of the issues the dimensions and
channels of the model raises. Looking at the second dimension of
the cube with younger, primary-age children; for example, the
'language across the curriculum' issue might be raised by asking,
'Are there any words we use in science, technology, history, etc. that
you don't understand?' What do pupils think about the subject
matter they are studying? Can they see any knowledge and skills
they are developing across the curriculum? For example, is the
information technology they learn in one subject category compat-
ible with, or contradictory to, what they learn in other subjects?
What about teaching and learning? Do they have the same modes
of learning and teaching in all subjects or is there variety, from their
vantage point?

Bibliography

Anderson, H.H. (1939) 'The measurement of domination and of socially integrative behaviour in teachers' contacts with children', *Child Development* 10: 73–89.

Ashton, P., Kneen, P. and Davies, F. (1975) *Aims into Practice in the Primary School*, London: Hodder & Stoughton.

Ausubel, D.P., Novak, J.D. and Hanesian, H. (1978) *Educational Psychology: A Cognitive View*, New York: Holt, Rinehart & Winston.

Bandura, A. (1977) *Social Learning Theory*, Englewood Cliffs, NJ: Prentice-Hall.

Bantock, G.H. (1980) *Dilemmas of the Curriculum*, Oxford: Martin Robertson.

Bennett, N., Desforges, C., Cockburn, A. and Wilkinson, B. (1984) *The Quality of Pupil Learning Experiences*, London: Lawrence Erlbaum Associates.

Bloom, B.S. (1956) *Taxonomy of Educational Objectives*, New York: Longman.

Brown, G.A. and Wragg, E.C. (1993) *Questioning*, London: Routledge.

Bruner, J.S. (1960) *The Process of Education*, Cambridge, MA: Harvard University Press.

Clay, M.M. (1985) *The Early Detection of Reading Difficulties: A Diagnostic Survey with Recovery Procedures*, 2nd edn, Exeter, NH: Heinemann.

Dearden, R.F. (1976) *Problems in Primary Education*, London: Routledge & Kegan Paul.

Denham, C. and Lieberman, A. (1980) *Time to Learn*, Washington: National Institute of Education.

Dewey, J. (1938) *Experience and Education*, New York: Collier/Macmillan.

Dunne, E. and Bennett, N. (1990) *Talking and Learning in Groups*, Basingstoke: Macmillan.

—— (1996) 'The acquisition of core skills in higher education and employment', in K. Percy, (ed.) *Towards a Learning Workforce* (Papers from a conference held in September 1995 at Lancaster University), Lancaster: Lancaster University.

Feuerstein, R. (1980) *Instrumental Enrichment: An Intervention Program for Cognitive Modifiability*, Baltimore, MD: University Park Press.

Gage, N.L. and Berliner, D.C. (1984) *Educational Psychology*, Boston: Houghton Mifflin Co.

Hamilton, D. (1975) 'Handling innovation in the classroom: two case studies' in W.A. Reid and D.F. Walker (eds) *Case Studies in Curriculum Change*, London: Routledge.

Handy, C. (1994) *The Empty Raincoat: Making Sense of the Future*, London: Hutchinson.

Harrison, C. and Nicoll, A. (1984) 'The readability of health care literature', *Developmental Medicine and Child Neurology*, 26: 588–95.

Her Majesty's Inspectorate (HMI) (1977) *Curriculum 11–16*, London: HMSO.

—— (1985) *The Curriculum from 5–16*, London: HMSO.

Hirst, P.H. (1974) *Knowledge and the Curriculum*, London: Routledge & Kegan Paul.

Hughes, M. (1983) 'What is difficult about learning arithmetic?' in M. Donaldson, R. Grieve, and C.J. Pratt. *Early Childhood Development and Education*, Oxford: Blackwell.

Hutton, W. (1995) *The State We're In*, London: Jonathan Cape.

Lipman, M. (1991) *Thinking in Education*, Cambridge, MA: Harvard University Press.

Piaget, J. (1954) *The Construction of Reality in the Child*, New York: Basic Books.

Plowden Report, DES (1967) *Children and their Primary Schools*, Report of the Central Advisory Council for Education, London: HMSO.

Posner, G. (1995) *Analyzing the Curriculum*, 2nd edn, New York: McGraw-Hill.

Purves, A. (1971) 'Evaluation of learning in literature', in B.S. Bloom, J.T. Hastings and G.F. Madaus (eds) *Handbook on Formative and Summative Evaluation of Student Learning*, New York: McGraw-Hill.

Radnor, H.A. (1994) *Across the Curriculum*, London: Cassell.

Ryle, G. (1949) *The Concept of Mind*, London: Hutchinson.

Schmuck, R.A. and Schmuck, P.A. (1975) *Group Processes in the Classroom*, Dubuque, IA: William C. Brown Co.

Schoen, D. (1983) *The Reflective Practitioner*, New York: Basic Books

Shayer, M. (1996) 'Piaget and Vygotsky: a necessary marriage for effective educational intervention', in L. Smith. (ed.) *Critical Readings on Piaget* (forthcoming), London: Routledge.

Speaker's Commission (1990) *Encouraging Citizenship*, London: HMSO.

Stenhouse, L. (1975) *An Introduction to Curriculum Research and Development*, London: Heinemann.

Taba, H., Durkin, M.C., Fraenkel, J.R. and McNaughton, A.H. (1971) *A Teacher's Handbook to Elementary Social Studies*, 2nd edn, Reading MA: Addison-Wesley.

Vygotsky, L. (1978) *Mind in Society*, London: Harvard University Press.

Wang, M.C., Haertel, G.D. and Walberg, H.J. (1993) 'Toward a knowledge base for school learning', *Review of Educational Research* 63: 249–94.

Wilcox, B. and Eustace, P.J. (1980) *Tooling up for Curriculum Review*, Windsor: NFER.

Wittgenstein, L. (1922) *Tractatus Logico-Philosophicus*.

Wragg, E.C. (ed.) (1984) *Classroom Teaching Skills*, London: Croom Helm.

—— (1993) *Primary Teaching Skills*, London: Routledge.

Wragg, E.C. and Brown, G.A. (1993) *Explaining*, London: Routledge.

Wragg, E.C. (1996) *Billy's Guides*, in Wragg, E.C. (ed.) *Taking Flight*, Walton on Thames: Thomas Nelson.

Index